THE
NEIGHBORHOOD EMERGENCY RESPONSE
HANDBOOK

YOUR LIFESAVING PLAN FOR PERSONAL AND COMMUNITY PREPAREDNESS

SCOTT FINAZZO

Ulysses Press

To my mother, Theresa Lopez. I've never had to worry about believing in myself because she has always believed in me enough for both of us.

❖

Published in the U.S. by
Ulysses Press
P.O. Box 3440
Berkeley, CA 94703
www.ulyssespress.com

ISBN: 978-1-61243-453-7
Library of Congress Control Number 2014952011

Printed in Canada by Marquis Book Printing

10 9 8 7 6 5 4 3 2 1

Acquisitions Editor: Keith Riegert
Managing Editor: Claire Chun
Editor: Renee Rutledge
Proofreader: Lauren Harrison
Cover design: Noah Mercer
Interior design and layout: Jake Flaherty
Photo credits: page 176
Models: Doug Hall, Micah Jensen, Rick Maggio, Mike Morgan,
    Terra Moriarty, Xavier Panimboza,

Distributed by Publishers Group West

CONTENTS

INTRODUCTION

Emergency services provide a security blanket under which we all live. If we need a fire truck, a police car, or an ambulance, we can simply call 911 and they are immediately dispatched to mediate whatever has caused us alarm. It is a convenience that we hope never to need, but when we do, help is most certainly on the way. But what if it isn't?

Times and circumstances may arise when emergency responders can become overwhelmed and the need for help exceeds the resources available. It can happen anywhere. No one is immune to disaster. It finds its way into the most populated cities and the farthest remote regions of the country. A winter storm, tornado, wildfire, hurricane, flood, or even civil unrest can disable a community and bring social services to a halt. Those left in its wake may be forced to become self-reliant for a period of time. It is during those critical hours or days when essential and sometimes lifesaving actions are necessary. Training and a basic understanding of the principles involved during a disaster response can mean the difference between becoming a victim, being a spectator, or contributing to a positive outcome following the event.

Though the focus of this book is primarily disaster response, you will find that a common theme is preparation. As the son of a firefighter and having been in the fire service for nearly 20 years myself, I cannot stress the importance of preparation enough. Firefighters constantly train and prepare for potential encounters. A firefighter may never have to fight a fire in a high-rise building, but you can be certain if a tall building is in their response area, he or she knows how. A firefighter may never have to respond to a child who was playing on a frozen pond and fell through the ice, but if you live in a place where temperatures drop below freezing, your local firefighters will be ready if it happens. The fire service is ever vigilant and a large part of that is in being prepared.

How you respond begins with how you prepare. When a crisis occurs, your brain draws from survival instinct and past experiences to formulate your reaction. You have bookmarks in your brain that, without thinking, you call upon to dictate how to respond to a situation. That's not to say that just because you have never had to endure a hurricane you'll be helpless when it happens. Your brain will automatically call upon experiences you've had, whether they were real-life incidents or past training, to guide your response. Gaining that knowledge and experience before the disaster occurs, effectively giving your brain a playbook, is probably the most important method to ensure you are ready when it comes time to respond.

In the Midwest, where I work as a firefighter, we are prone to severe thunderstorms, tornados, blizzards, flooding, and even civil unrest. On several occasions, we've found ourselves in the fire truck doing everything we could to reach everyone who needed help, but have been limited by time, tools, or terrain. It can be a struggle just getting down the street sometimes because of storm debris. It is extremely frustrating when that happens because the calls for help aren't just items on a to-do list—they are people are waiting for help. Oftentimes, those people will do what they have to for safety and survival until help arrives. It is for that reason that I wanted to write this book. In desperate times, I want you to have the proper tools in your mental and physical toolbox to be able to keep yourself and your family safe. You, your experience, and your training, along with the cooperation of those around you, can be the only means of providing safety for a prolonged period.

Examples upon examples abound of communities banding together to help each other following a crisis. I've seen some of the most amazing acts of humanity take place during the darkest hours. An alliance is formed through shared experience and survival. At such a time, your neighbor is not your neighbor, but an extension of yourself. You feel a sense of responsibility toward them and vice versa.

Community based disaster response began with the Los Angeles Fire Department (LAFD) in 1985, when city officials traveled to Mexico City following a major earthquake. They witnessed volunteer rescuers save over 800 people. This prompted the city of Los Angeles to develop a pilot program to train citizens in preparation, survival, and recovery. The program was accelerated following the Whittier Narrows earthquake of 1987, when the LAFD took an active role training its citizens by creating the Disaster Preparedness Division that trained communities and companies to meet their immediate needs following a disaster. After a crisis occurs, people rally together to help others who were affected. You've seen it on the news: survivors joining forces to help their fellow man. Sadly, because the majority of people are ill-prepared to undergo the mental and physical demands of the dangerous conditions placed upon them, spontaneous volunteers experience additional injuries and even death.

Organized community response began to take shape in earnest following the Loma Prieta earthquake that occurred on October 17, 1989. You may remember watching its aftermath on the small screen, as it was the first nationally televised earthquake in the United States. It struck just before the start of game three of the World Series, which was taking place at Candlestick Park in San Francisco. The quake measured 6.9 on the Richter scale and caused mass destruction over a large area near the central California coast. The cities of San Francisco, Los Altos, Santa Cruz, Oakland, and other surrounding areas saw mass destruction, numerous casualties, vast power outages, communication blackouts, and crippled transportation. Emergency response crews were inundated with calls for help that far exceeded their capacity. Untrained and unprepared people were forced to fend for themselves until help could arrive.

In the months following the earthquake, the San Francisco Fire Department developed a training program called NERT (neighborhood emergency response team). NERT was intended to reach out to the community and offer citizens the self-confidence and skills to increase their safety and well-being after a disaster. By 1993, the Federal Emergency Management Agency, or FEMA, adopted a similar program called CERT (community emergency response team), and by 2012 CERT programs were being offered in all 50 states, including Washington, D.C., and Puerto Rico. NERT and CERT programs are hosted by a sponsoring agency that organizes and trains citizens, providing a coordinated network of volunteer responders who have received similar training in first aid, disaster response, and incident command structure.

In training, those volunteers obtain many of the same skills and philosophies you will learn in this book. I taught CERT for many years through my fire department and appreciate the interest and dedication that the students, and you, have to help ensure your community is ready for a disaster. I recall students walking into class for the first time, their ages ranging from 18 to 80, each one as eager to learn as the next. The common thread among them was their desire to take care of their families and community. Each student was there not only to avoid becoming a victim, but more importantly, to be able to help those who can't help themselves—to be proactive rather than reactive. That was the inspiration for this book: getting the necessary information in the hands of those who want to be a part of the solution in the direst of circumstances.

My hope is that you will use this book as a resource and a foundation for your own emergency preparedness and response. I have worked hard to make *The Neighborhood Emergency Response Handbook* as inclusive as possible. After reading this book, I encourage you to take a closer look at your surroundings. View your home, workplace, school, church, or any other place that you frequent with a different perspective. Identify the locations of first aid and safety equipment. Take inventory of safe areas and exits. Consider what resources you have available to you, your evacuation route options, and what supplies you may need. Take what you have learned and apply it to those areas of your life where you and your family spend the most time. Personalize the information you have obtained and the skills you have learned. Most of all, make certain you are prepared to take care of yourself and those around you.

CHAPTER 1
WHEN DISASTER STRIKES

A disastrous event occurs—one that alters your typical way of life and places you in a situation where you are forced to react. It could be a natural disaster, a man-made catastrophe, or a weather-related incident as common as a severe storm. The event itself, for now, is irrelevant. You and your family have been placed in harm's way and are left reeling in its wake. Under normal circumstances, you would call 911 and emergency responders would immediately be sent in to mitigate the crisis. But this isn't a "normal circumstance." This is a disaster. Help is on the way, but who knows how long it will take to arrive. So, for the time being, you must provide aid, offer assistance, and take emergency actions. But where to begin? What would the professionals do?

INCIDENT PRIORITIES

Due to the vast range of possible incident calls that emergency responders answer, their decision-making process can be overwhelming. Destruction, fire, flooding, medical issues, and any number of other obstacles hamper their efforts to bring calm to a chaotic situation. In order to simplify their actions they utilize three *incident priorities:* life safety, incident stabilization, and property conservation. That phrase makes them sound very official and stringent and, although these priorities can and should be used in every emergency scenario, they are often employed without conscious premeditation.

Life safety is and should always be your first priority in any kind of emergency. There is no bigger concern than the lives of the victims and the responders. Given any situation, most "victims" will self-rescue if possible. Self-preservation is our most primal instinct and will engage without conscious thought. Those who can't remove themselves from harm in a disaster scenario should be the utmost priority, second only to your own safety. It does not sound heroic to say, but by becoming a casualty yourself, you only compound the problem.

Incident stabilization is the second priority. Incident stabilization is a fancy way of saying to *stop a bad thing from getting worse.* Stabilizing an incident can occur in a variety of ways. It can mean shutting off a gas meter, putting out a fire, or shoring up a weakened structure. When it comes to dealing with the weather, unfortunately, stabilization isn't an option. You must ensure you are prepared, sustain the event, and then recover.

Although incident priorities should *always* be addressed in order, sometimes they can occur concurrently. There are times when, by stabilizing the incident, you protect lives by doing so. For example, putting out a small fire prevents it from becoming a large fire that endangers many lives. You have stabilized the incident, and in turn, protected lives.

Property conservation is the third and final incident priority. Emergency responders care about your property: your home, keepsakes, important documents, irreplaceable items, etc. Those items can and should be addressed, but *only* once lives are no longer in jeopardy and incident stabilization has occurred. When it is deemed safe to do so, you can retrieve pictures, birth certificates, family heirlooms, and other assorted items.

ACCOUNTABILITY

Typically, when a crisis occurs, people and things are scattered. Homes and buildings are destroyed or, at the very least, compromised, and the people within them have either self-evacuated, were forcefully removed, or are trapped within. It is not unusual for all three to have happened. That's why it is critical to have some measure of accounting for your loved ones' status and whereabouts

The very best way to ensure accountability is preparation. If your family is forced to evacuate your home and everyone goes a different direction, accountability has been lost. The first piece of information that anyone responding or wishing to help will require is if everyone is safe. If not, locating, protecting, and performing rescues becomes their first priority. Unfortunately, bystanders and responders have risked and lost their own lives to locate someone who was later found to be safe but simply unaccounted for.

Ideally accountability happens before, during, *and* after an incident.

Before an emergency situation occurs, you should make sure everyone around you is together, safe, and prepared. With sufficient warning comes the ability to prepare and, in keeping with our incident priorities, our first task is to account for those around us. At home we account for our family members and guests. At work we account for our coworkers and visitors. In public places such as churches, department stores, and theaters, accountability becomes a bit more of a challenge and comes down to visual observation: *Is everyone around me safe?*

This all assumes sufficient warning. There are times when, often tragically, there isn't, and timely accountability after the incident is a chaotic and lofty goal. It may be unknown whether your family, friends, or coworkers have evacuated or are trapped somewhere. Those are the situations when a pre-established accountability plan is critical, because you must react to an immediate and perilous circumstance.

During the incident, keep everyone as a group if possible. When there is little or no warning, knowing where your family, coworkers, or friends are may not be feasible. For example, if a fire occurs in your home or if, for whatever reason, your office building suffers structural collapse, you won't have the opportunity to conduct a roll call beforehand. You must evacuate or protect yourself and those around you and then attempt to account for everyone else at the earliest possible opportunity. When you have had sufficient warning, accountability should become easier as everyone is ideally together in a safe location. Again, rescue is based on accountability. The more people for whom you can account, the less risk that must be taken to locate and assist those in need.

After the event, take a quick inventory of those around you. Begin with those in close proximity and work your way out. Can you account for your family, friends, coworkers, or anyone else who was near to you during the incident? Once you have deemed that you and those closest to you are safe, you can begin to check the welfare of others.

CHOOSE A MEETING PLACE

Children are taught at an early age to have a "meeting place." A meeting place is a safe place outside of the home where family members can convene to ensure accountability after a crisis. Identify a meeting place near your home. It should be as safe a location as possible. The meeting place should also be nearby, easily accessible, and in a spot where you will be able to make contact with responders once they arrive. Make sure everyone in the family is aware of the meeting place and practice going there.

DISASTERS AT HOME

Disasters can happen anytime, anywhere, to anyone. A disaster at your home is likely the most devastating scenario. All that you have worked for and made your own takes a hit. At home, it's personal. It is YOUR family's safety being compromised. It is YOUR home sustaining the damage. It is

YOUR belongings that are at risk of being lost, damaged, or destroyed. You are physically, financially, and psychologically under attack.

The positive aspect to a disaster happening at home is the benefit of homefield advantage. You should have emergency supplies already prepared. You are intimately aware of the details of the structure itself (construction type, materials used, strengths, weaknesses, protected areas, etc.) and have identified what resources are available to you. The greatest benefit is familiarization with your surroundings.

Part of your preparation prior to a disaster should be familiarization with local warning systems. Authorities will give you as much warning as possible to prepare for a disaster. They also have ways to communicate when the event is over and you are safe to leave your sheltered area. Make sure you have a way (weather radio, telephone capabilities, etc.) of knowing when it is safe to begin taking inventory of people and evaluating the damage.

SIZE-UP

Size-up is another term used by responders to get an overall perspective of any situation to better decide on a course of action. It is getting the big picture. When a significant event has happened, it is easy to become drawn in to what visually appears as its worst aspect. In the medical field this is called a *distracting injury:* You notice the person with the severely mangled hand who is screaming loudly and immediately focus your attention to it, failing to notice the other person who sustained a head injury and is losing consciousness. The most important part of performing a good size-up is to take in as much information as you can and then, based on the incident priorities, act.

Before you act, ask yourself three questions: What has happened? What is happening now? What is going to happen? A good size-up will draw from all SIX of your senses, the sixth one being your instinct.

Sight: What do you see? What is the extent of the damage? Are there injured or trapped victims? Are you in a safe area or should you relocate?

Hearing: Is anyone yelling for help? Can you hear gas leaking or water running? Do you hear approaching sirens?

Smell: Do you smell smoke, natural gas, or any other suspicious odors?

Touch: Is something hot to the touch? Cold to the touch? Abnormal? Weakened? Broken? Is the rain or wind picking up?

Taste: Believe it or not there are taste receptors located in the smooth muscles of your trachea and bronchi. If you have an odd taste in your mouth with no reasonable explanation, that may be a warning that you have inhaled an irritant of some kind. Consider the possible hazard and evacuate to a safer location.

Instinct: Trust it, even if there is no other obvious evidence suggesting you take or avoid a course of action. Stress can deteriorate your ability to perceive what is going on around you. The hormones released in your body during a stressful situation can interfere with your brain's ability to see, hear, and pick up environmental cues. While all of this is happening, you may simply have a gut feeling. Your instinct could quite possibly be the subconscious recognition of something that has pushed through the chemical whirlwind happening inside of you.

Another part of size-up is prediction. Using your best judgment, based on the information you have obtained, you will want to forecast what will likely happen. You don't need to be expertly trained. It's a simple analysis of a situation and predicting what you think may happen. This could mean the difference between risky action and the safety of inaction. For example, imagine that a flood has occurred and a vehicle has stalled out as the raging water swells above the tires, almost to the windows. The driver has climbed out, onto the roof, and is now yelling madly for help. Even rescuers would tell you that entering fast-moving water is an extremely risky action. Before you emotionally react and jump into the water in a likely futile rescue attempt, you take a moment and evaluate the situation. In doing so, you learn that the rain is stopping and water levels have peaked and are dropping. So, rather than becoming a potentially second victim, you wait mere minutes, the water level drops, and the driver walks through ankle deep water to safety.

All of these observations and questions should factor in to an overall plan created from your size-up. If time and the situation allows, it's not a bad idea to share your size-up with someone else. They may have information or experience that you do not have. Once you have performed a good size-up, you can decide on a course of action that includes where, who, and how to respond.

THE NINE STEPS OF A SIZE-UP

1. Gather facts. What has happened? How many people have been killed, injured, or affected (generally speaking—specifics aren't critical at this point)?

2. Assess damage. What is the magnitude? Is one building affected? Multiple buildings? An entire city? Consider what has happened compared to what is happening now.

3. Consider probabilities. What is likely to happen next? Is the situation getting better or worse? How will your actions affect the outcome?

4. Assess your situation. Are you in immediate danger? Do you have adequate training and equipment needed to offer assistance?

5. Establish priorities. Using the incident priorities (life safety, incident stabilization, property conservation), determine how you can do the greatest good for the greatest number of people.

6. Make decisions. Take all of the information you have obtained in steps 1 to 5 and decide your goals.

7. Develop a plan of action. Determine a plan that is in accordance with the incident priorities and accomplishes your goals. Simple plans can be verbal, but more complex plans should be written down. Communicate the plan clearly to those who are assisting you.

8. Take action. Execute your plan and be prepared to report the situation accurately to emergency responders as they arrive.

9. Evaluate progress. Take the time, at regular intervals, to evaluate your progress and determine if your goals are being met or if a deviation from the plan is needed.

UTILITY SHUT-OFF

Your home, whether it is a single family house or a unit in a high-rise apartment building, utilizes a combination of utilities: gas, electricity, and water. Many homes contain all three, and at the very least likely contain water and electricity. These utilities offer us many of the comforts we enjoy daily and often take for granted. During a disaster or extreme weather event, your house may incur structural damage. One of the first things you may need to do if your home sustains any kind of destruction is to shut off your utilities. A broken water pipe, leaking natural gas, and electrical arcing all present their share of potentially deadly issues. Having the knowledge and ability to turn them off is essential.

Other more unique options potentially found in your home include solar electricity or propane, but this section will focus on the most common: gas, electricity, and water. If you are not familiar with them, shutting off your utilities can be a confusing and stressful task, especially when the need is immediate. Before the situation arises you should identify what is specific to your home and prepare accordingly. In some situations the valves are in odd places or require special tools to operate. Know where the utilities enter your home and, more importantly, where and how to turn them off.

Locating utility shut-offs in a single family home is a much easier task than finding them in an apartment building or high-rise. If you live in a multi-family structure with apartments or condos, you should contact your building maintenance representative and ask for a few minutes of their time to learn where and how to shut off utilities to your building.

Water

Broken water pipes happen all too often due to freezing and thawing in the winter months of cold climates. They are also common to most every kind of natural disaster. Whatever the cause, a broken water pipe in the home can cause a wide variety of problems that include drowning, electrical hazards, and long-term wood rot and mold problems.

There are several ways to shut off your residential water.

1. The first and simplest way is to locate the shut-off valve where the water line enters your house. In warmer climates the shut-off valve may be located outside of your home where the water line meets the exterior. In the majority of climates it will be located just inside the house where the water line comes in through the foundation or wall.

Note: If your water comes in through a ground well, the valves on either side of the pressure tank should both be shut off.

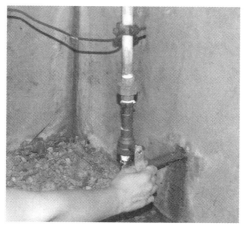

Locate the shut-off valve where the water line enters the house.

2. The water shut-off valve should be a quarter-turn ball valve. If you have this type of setup, you simply turn the valve a quarter of a turn until it is perpendicular to the water pipe. In some homes the valve has a round handle, in which case you would turn the handle clockwise until you can't turn it anymore. Simple to find. Simple to do.

3. If you don't have a master shut-off valve to your home (it is strongly recommended you have one installed) you can also turn the water off at the municipal water meter shut-off valve typically located in your front or side yard. You will find a round metal lid or box, usually located near a property boundary line, anywhere from 24 to 48 inches from the curb or fence line.

Water can be shut off to a home or a commercial building by locating the water meter outside, often in the ground in front of the structure.

- Round metal lid: If your water meter has a round metal lid you can use a wrench or a pair of pliers to rotate the lone nut on the lid counterclockwise to release the latch and open. Another type of metal lid requires you to insert a screwdriver and turn the lid until the tabs line up with the gaps, allowing you to lift it off.

- Square or rectangular lid: Insert a screwdriver or pry bar and pry open.

Before reaching into the meter box, inspect the area for debris or rodents. Various kinds of valves that turn off the water to your home will be found inside. Regardless of which type of home you live in, the principle will be the same. You will need a pair of pliers or a specialty tool to turn the valve until it is perpendicular to the water pipe and the water is shut off.

Keep in mind that you may not necessarily need to shut off water to the entire house. Most newer houses should have shut-off valves installed at every sink and toilet in the home and several at the water heater in case you are able to simply localize your water issue.

Electricity

Electricity is woven throughout your home, reaching into nearly every wall of every room. It is safely contained within those walls and we reap the benefits, without thought, every single day. When the electricity is no longer safely encapsulated it becomes extremely dangerous—even deadly.

A live wire can cause electrical shock or death and even the slightest spark can ignite leaking natural gas. If electricity has become a danger in your house, you should immediately shut off your power.

1. If the electrical panel is damaged or there is standing water near the breaker box, evacuate immediately and deny entry. Otherwise, the first thing you will need to do is locate your main breaker panel. Vast possibilities of electrical panels and shut-offs exist. Nearly all homes will have a single electrical feed while multi-family buildings could have several. In most homes the panel will be located in the basement or a utility room.

2. Make sure everyone in your home knows where the breaker panel is located.

3. Identify the "main" circuit breaker. You can shut off power to only certain parts of your house with individual circuit breakers, isolating a small electrical issue, but the easiest and safest thing to do is to shut off the main breaker, disabling electricity to the entire house. The main shut-off is usually located at the top of the breaker panel and should be labeled.

4. Simply flip the main switch to "off." If you cannot locate the main shut-off, you can individually flip all the breaker switches on the panel to the off position.

5. Keep in mind that shutting off the main breaker only discontinues power to the inside wiring of your home. The line coming into your house will still be live.

Natural Gas

Natural gas has many residential and commercial benefits but can be incredibly dangerous. Following a disaster, natural gas leaks are responsible for a significant number of fires and explosions. It doesn't always require a major event to cause a leak. For homes that utilize natural gas, it is even common, during especially dry summers, for the soil near the foundation to shift, causing the gas meter to move. Often this results in damaged and leaking gas lines. Homes and buildings can have different gas meter configurations, so it is important to locate your meter and shut-off before the emergency arises. It is recommended that you contact your local gas company and learn about their recommendations and procedures for shutting off the natural gas to your house or building.

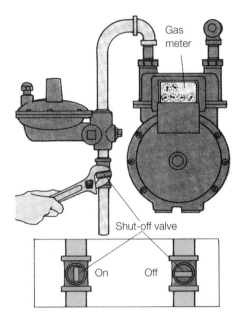

1. If you hear hissing and smell the slightest hint of natural gas, you should evacuate the home and contact the gas company immediately. In the event of a disaster, when a response from the gas company is likely delayed, you should open windows and shut the gas off at the meter.

2. Natural gas meters will typically be located outside and right next to your house. Locate the shut-off valve next to the meter on the inlet pipe and turn it a quarter of a turn using a crescent wrench or an emergency gas shut-off wrench until it is perpendicular to the pipe.

3. Once gas is shut off, it should only be turned back on by a professional.

CARBON MONOXIDE

Carbon monoxide (CO) is one of the most insidious elements found in your home. It is a colorless, tasteless, and odorless gas that can cause sudden illness and death. It is virtually undetectable except for when medical symptoms occur or with a functioning CO detector.

Carbon monoxide is the byproduct of the incomplete combustion of materials containing carbon, which means it can be produced by virtually anything that burns, such as natural gas, coal, wood, fuel oil, and charcoal. The most common sources of CO in a residence are gas-powered appliances. (Other sources include vehicle exhaust in attached garages, gas space heaters, woodstoves, fireplaces, and even tobacco smoke.) It is important to know that while gas-powered appliances are a primary source of CO, if they are maintained and operating properly, carbon monoxide should

A carbon monoxide detector, preferably one with a digital display, provides you the best method of early detection of CO in the home.

not be a significant threat. Problems arise when there is a malfunction, improper installation, neglected maintenance, or inadequate ventilation. During a dangerous weather event or natural disaster, where the structure of your home has been affected, it is very possible to have carbon monoxide present in your house.

THE DANGER

CO mixes evenly with air. Therefore, regardless of where the source may be, it is dispersed to all parts of your home by the HVAC system. Once it has permeated your air and is inadvertently inhaled, carbon monoxide displaces oxygen in the body's red blood cells. Oxygen is obviously vital for life and if the cells cannot absorb it, rapid illness and death can occur.

Since carbon monoxide is the byproduct of incomplete combustion, flammability is not really an issue. The primary danger of CO is medical. As it is picked up by the red blood cells, symptoms such as confusion, headache, dizziness, weakness, nausea, vomiting, and chest pain occur, followed by loss of consciousness and death. People who are asleep or intoxicated may not be able to recognize that they are symptomatic.

That is why a CO detector is so vitally important. Even a single detector can be the difference between life and death.

One of the most important measures of prevention you can do to prevent CO poisoning is to ensure all of your gas-powered appliances are in good working order and properly maintained. Next, purchase a CO detector. They can be found at any local department or hardware store. Experts recommend one with a battery backup and digital display so you can not only know if the detector has activated, but know the amount of carbon monoxide being detected. (The instruction manual will tell you what the associated readings mean.) If your detector activates, call 911. If you do not have a detector and one or more people in the home have unexplained symptoms, leave the house and call 911. In either case, you should then get out of the house. Immediate fresh air is required. An expert will be needed to identify the source of the leak.

PERSONAL SAFETY

After a disaster, turmoil ensues. Structures become damaged, people are injured, and order gives way to chaos and survival. Those who sustained the event, whose personal safety often takes a backseat to their instinct to assure the safety of others, are commonly unprepared and poorly supplied. Therefore, take steps to ensure your own safety before the event.

You should have readily available items on hand to ensure your own personal safety. The Center for Disease Control (CDC) recommends that five areas of personal protective equipment (PPE) be addressed: respirators, protective clothing, protection from skin exposure, eye protection, and hearing protection. To give yourself the best possible security in a hazardous and unstable environment, store items in each category.

Your predisaster personal safety comes in the form of supplies, education, and insurance. Although not necessary for survival, insurance plays a strong role in your post-disaster recovery. Homeless with a collection of insurmountable medical bills is no way to begin your rebuilding process. Prepare your home by making sure that it has adequate insurance and that insurance covers all of the things that you think may damage your home. Many natural disasters such as wildfires and flooding will require extra insurance that you have to specifically add to your plan.

In your home, and maybe even in your personal vehicle, you should stock supplies to help keep you safe. Common safety supplies to include are:

- Appropriate footwear
- Flashlights
- Food
- Hard hat
- Knife
- Leather gloves
- Medical supplies
- Safety glasses
- Sunscreen
- Utility shut-off tools
- Weather radio

Education is a vital part of personal safety. It is obtained in classes and books, gained by practice, and solidified in experience. Education begins when you take the initiative to learn more. Sign up for first aid, CPR classes, and community emergency response classes. Those types of classes offer the dual benefit of teaching a new skill as well as putting you in contact with like-minded people with whom to form community networks. In addition to attending classes, read literature, watch videos, and talk to experts. Expose yourself to as much information as possible and practice your skills.

PETS

They are as much a part of our family as anyone and depend on us for their well-being. Our pets, unfortunately, can be forgotten when it comes to disasters. Ideally we have made the appropriate preparations for them just as we have for our family members. All too often, this isn't the case and pets become helpless victims. As a pet owner it is your responsibility to not only ensure they are prepared for a disaster, but to keep them safe in its wake.

Before a Crisis

The first step you can take to prepare your pet is to ensure immunizations are up to date and they have a collar or some type of clear and current identification that includes contact information. In 2005, during Hurricane Katrina, nearly 200,000 pets were reportedly displaced. If you and your pets become separated, proper contact information can help expedite reuniting you with your companion.

The next step is to identify a safe evacuation area. A situation may arise that forces you to make a choice: shelter in place or evacuate. When deciding whether to stay home or to evacuate, your pets warrant forethought and consideration. If you must evacuate your home, take your pets with you. Their chance for survival greatly increases if you are able to take them when you leave. Despite "animal instinct," domesticated pets rely on us for their safety and are unlikely to survive on their own. During a crisis people often evacuate to storm shelters. Bringing your pet with you can complicate the situation. Most shelters do not allow pets, so if you are going to evacuate to a shelter, it is imperative that you check first to ensure that pets are permitted. You should locate pet-friendly shelters or hotels, particularly along your evacuation route.

Then you will want to make preparations in your home. Many of the same items you would set aside for your family to utilize in the event of a disaster should also be considered for your pets.

When discussing pets, we are most commonly referring to dogs and cats. Your pet could be anything from a goldfish to a horse. The important thing is to have items ready in advance to care for them, regardless of size. Your preparations should include:

- At least a three-day supply of food and water
- A pet first aid guide and appropriate supplies
- A leash or harness allowing you to contain a confused or frightened animal
- A carrier or cage large enough for your pet to stand comfortably and turn around in
- Waste cleanup supplies
- Comfort items such as toys or a blanket
- Copies of medical records, including a current picture of your pet

After a Crisis

After a crisis, your pet is going to be stressed and afraid, even if you are able to remain home throughout. Familiar scenery and scents may have changed, potentially causing confusion and altered behavior. Disorientation and fear may cause them to run away. Keep them close. Larger household pets should be fenced or leashed to both comfort and protect them. Keeping them in familiar surroundings reduces stress and helps to ensure their safety. It also reduces their risk of coming in contact with potentially dangerous animals that have been displaced due to the event.

Keep your pets from drinking standing water after a disaster. The water could contain any number of hazardous materials or bacteria. Just as with your family members, your pets should drink bottled water until the authorities deem that tap water is safe to drink.

Exotic pets such as lizards, snakes, and frogs present unique issues. Cold-blooded animals that usually utilize a warming lamp will need some kind of alternative method to keep warm. Consider what your pet will need before the crisis.

Disease

You should take special precautions dealing with animals following a disaster, when the spread of disease is common. Your pets can be exposed to a variety of things that could make them sick. Some of these illnesses can be transmitted to people. Be aware of:

- Rabies, which affects the nervous system and is transmitted by a bite from an infected animal.

- Ringworm is a fungus that can affect the skin, hair, and nails of both humans and animals. It is transmitted from animals to people by way of direct contact with the animal or contact with something the animal has touched.

- Leptospirosis is a bacterial disease that is spread by contact with the urine of an infected animal or contaminated water, food, or soil. It can cause significant kidney damage.

- Fleas, ticks, and mosquitoes can transmit a variety of diseases and infections from animal to human.

Many of these can be avoided by ensuring your pet is up to date on its vaccinations, washing your hands before and after pet contact, keeping your pet away from other animals (both within your household and outside of it), using preventative flea and tick treatments, and contacting your vet and/or physician if you suspect any infection has been obtained.

EVACUATION PREPAREDNESS

Whether it is a man-made disaster or an extreme weather event, the situation may dictate that it is not safe to remain in your home. It happens more often than most people think. Hurricanes, floods, and fires force people out of danger zones to distant but safe locations. The thought of evacuating the safety and security of your home is an intimidating proposition. By leaving your house you effectively give up home field advantage. Your home has ALL of your supplies, clothing, food, water, shelter, and creature comforts that sustain you through a crisis. When you or the authorities decide that it is best for you to evacuate, it leaves little time to establish a plan. Being prepared in advance is crucial, especially if you live in an area prone to the need for evacuation.

The two keys for a successful emergency relocation are information and preparation.

Identify Potential Hazards. Your evacuation preparation begins with identifying what threats are common to your region. Do you live in a flood plain? Are wildfires common in your area? Is your home along the Atlantic or Gulf Coast, which seem to have a hurricane bull's-eye on them? Do you experience winter storms that could cripple your city for days, even weeks? There are a variety of reasons you may need to evacuate. Identify your threats and plan accordingly.

Determine Evacuation Routes. Notice "routes" is plural. By selecting a singular passage, you set yourself up for failure, for two reasons. First, the crisis itself could eliminate your intended evacuation route, leaving you scrambling to figure out a plan B amid turmoil. Second, if you are being evacuated, chances are that a great number of other people are as well, which clogs common evacuation routes, creating a frustrating and dangerous experience. Allow yourself multiple options when the time comes that you must leave your home.

Designate a Meeting Place. Meeting places are an important aspect of accountability. They are especially important if an evacuation is in order. As people flee the disaster area, either before or after the event, there should be a predetermined place to meet. On a typical day, your family is often geographically scattered throughout the area near your home. One may be at work, another at school, another at the gym, etc. If the event (whatever it may be) were to occur and you were all forced to evacuate the area, would you know where to meet up? With cellular communication likely being compromised, you may not be able to call or text each other. For every person in your family, there is likely a different idea of where a safe place to meet might be. Having the discussion before the event will eliminate the guesswork and confusion of wondering where everyone is evacuating. Considering the potential hazards in your area and your established evacuation routes, determine a good meeting place and then a backup to that location. It could be the house of a family member, a hotel, a state park, or anywhere that will be safe to go and await the arrival of others expected to be there. It is also a good idea to have a backup meeting place in case the first is inaccessible.

Have an Accountability System in Place. Appoint an out-of-the-area friend or relative to serve as your point of contact. Let them know when you're leaving, where you're going, and when you intend to arrive at your destination. They can inform others of your status and advise you of any outside information that you may not know. This also frees you from fielding calls and texts from concerned acquaintances when you should be focused on getting yourself to safety.

DISASTER COMMUNICATION PLAN

1. Establish an out-of-town point of contact.

2. Notify family and friends of your point of contact.

3. Ensure all contact information for family and friends is up to date and correct. Give this list to your point of contact.

4. Put a laminated "contact card" in your child's backpack with your contact information as well as that of your out-of-town contact.

5. Quality check contact information annually.

If you have someone in the home with special needs that will require assistance, you should make preparations in advance with neighbors or relatives who can help. The same can be said for large animals or anything else that will dictate the need for aid in an emergent situation. Have those avenues of support in place far ahead of the crisis.

Prepare a checklist of tasks and supplies to ensure you don't forget anything crucial. This chapter focuses on relocating to a safe home, shelter, or hotel. If you, by the situation or your own preference, will be living off the land, you will need much more training, practice, and supplies. That should be utilized as a last resort. Below is an example of what your checklist may include:

- Advise emergency contact of your plans
- Shut off utilities
- Leave one interior light on in major areas of the home (so emergency responders can see if there is fire or flood inside, or if any victims have been left behind)
- Lock doors and windows/secure the property
- Important documents (birth certificates, legal documents, passports, etc.)
- Cash (credit and debit cards may not be an option)
- Medication
- First aid kit
- Flashlights
- Toiletries
- Clothing
- Food
- Water
- Pet supplies (food, water, leash, toys, etc.)
- Sentimental items/small valuables
- Personal protective equipment (PPE) (respirator, hard hat, safety glasses, hearing protection, appropriate clothing, sturdy footwear, and gloves)

- Extra batteries

- Weather radio

- Recreational items (reading material, games, etc.)

The right information is crucial. You will need to know what, when, who, and where.

What: What is the event that is causing you to potentially evacuate? What are the dangers? What is the risk if you choose to stay?

When: When will it directly affect your home? How much time do you have to prepare yourself and your home before you must leave?

Who: Who is being evacuated? How many people are in that geographical area?

Where: Where is the event now? Where has it been? Where is it going? Where are people being evacuated? Will it affect my evacuation route? Where will you go?

These questions must be asked to afford you a safe evacuation. In certain situations, time does not allow for planning or consideration. You will have to evacuate immediately. But for the ones that do, you will be far better off if you have evaluated and prepared in advance.

VEHICLE CONSIDERATIONS

In a disaster situation, the importance of mobility cannot be understated. Our best, safest, and most familiar means of transportation is our personal vehicle driving over paved roads. Unfortunately, the typical means of getting around may not be an option. Perhaps a solar flare has rendered your car's combustion engine lifeless or a natural disaster has destroyed bridges and roads or at the very least left them impassible, by traditional means, because of the debris littering them. At some point either before, during, or after the crisis you will need to relocate, obtain supplies, or maybe even transport a victim and must evaluate your transportation options accordingly.

There are many factors to consider, the first of which is who will be traveling. The number of people/pets and any physical limitations they present can determine many things when you are deciding what your transportation options are. A young, physically fit person traveling alone has more options than those traveling in groups with a variety of personal health and fitness levels.

Your starting location versus your destination or destinations can lead you toward certain types of transportation that lend themselves to the distance you may need to travel and over what terrain. This information will dictate a vehicle that will adequately make the journey. Will you be traveling on land or by way of water? Do you live in a mountainous region? Due to weather or geography, is four-wheel drive necessary?

Whether you decide to evacuate ahead of a threat or your location becomes implausible to remain in, the method in which you choose to remove yourself and your family should be thoroughly evaluated. Listed below are examples of common evacuation vehicles to consider and a few of their pros and cons:

	PROS	CONS
PERSONAL VEHICLE	• Familiarity and reliability • Easy to maneuver • Low purchase price compared to loaded "bug out" vehicles • Good handling and maneuverability • Low center of gravity	• Most are two-wheel drive • Limited by availability of fuel • Low ground clearance • Lightweight vehicle suspension
MOTOR HOME	• All-encompassing (mobile and provides sleeping, cooking, and restroom capabilities) • Roomy and comfortable • Lots of storage areas • Relatively safe during an accident and offers a good vantage point for personal security	• Large and slow • Poor fuel efficiency • High center of gravity • Poor hazardous road handling
MOTORCYCLE	• Fuel efficient • High maneuverability • Dirt bike offers off-road options	• Only usable for one to two people • Little or no storage options • Poor hazardous road handling • Operator is exposed to the weather and other dangers • Uncomfortable over long distances • Increased risk of injury in a crash • Easily stolen or taken over by would-be attackers or frantic storm victims

	PROS	CONS
WATERCRAFT	• Offers an alternative evacuation method other than crowded paved roads • Sailboats and kayaks do not require fuel • Moderate to good amount of storage (depending on the watercraft type) • Watercraft evacuation offers you the option to utilize the water and all it has to offer (hydration, food, isolation, etc.)	• Must live near navigable water and have access to your watercraft • Requires better planning and more experience in navigating than other forms of transportation • Unless you are on the ocean, you are limited to river courses or the confines of a lake • Isolated from the assistance from others • Power boats are limited by the amount of accessible fuel • Onboard tools and maintenance items are essential

SUMMARY

When disaster strikes, the things that we take for granted are suddenly, and sometimes violently, taken from us. Shelter, running water, and even the simple comfort of knowing that your loved ones are safe are no longer guaranteed. It is then that you will know the benefits of preparation. Buying supplies, reading books, taking classes, or simply sitting around the kitchen table with your family to discuss what you would do during a catastrophic event puts you ahead of most. Too often the common attitude lies somewhere between "I should prepare one of these days" and "it probably won't happen to me." That paradigm is fine right up until the disaster happens.

All actions, whether performed before, during, or after the event, should revolve around safety. In this chapter, you learned the incident priorities: life safety, incident stabilization, and property conservation. These priorities provide the framework for the way you respond and the actions you take. It is one thing to read it in a book. It's another thing to experience a personal and life-threatening disaster firsthand. When I show up in the fire truck, almost without fail, I see people that have banded together to take care of each other. It is the sense of community and connectivity that brings out the best in people in the worst of circumstances. Forethought and preplanning will provide the best possible outcome for you and your community.

CHAPTER 2
BASIC DISASTER PROCEDURES

Depending on location, your region will be prone to specific weather-related threats. Tornados tear swaths across the Midwest. Hurricanes pound the shores of the Gulf Coast and eastern seaboard. Earthquakes shake the foundations of cities along the Pacific Ocean. People who live in those areas are all too familiar with the peril that natural disasters bring. This chapter highlights several of these disaster types and specific preparations that can and should be done to ready your family and your home.

Included as well are preparations and procedures for civil unrest. We live in a tumultuous time and have seen disorder rear its ugly head all over the world. More specifically and more frightening is that it can and has happened in big cities and small towns all across our nation.

These lists are meant to be a starting point. Personalize the lists and expand on them to better suit your family's needs. No one knows your specific demands better than you do. Customize your own home and preparations to ensure you will be ready for a disaster and will know the procedures to follow in the aftermath of everything from a flood, storm, or blizzard to an earthquake, tornado, or civil unrest.

CREATING A DISASTER KIT

FEMA offers recommendations for building an emergency supply kit in advance of any disaster that will help sustain you and your family for a minimum of three days. Of course, the disaster supply kit that you build should be based on your specific wants and needs, as well as the duration of time that you would like to be prepared. For the sake of getting started, below are some of the items recommended by FEMA. This will provide you with the foundation for building your personal disaster kit to help prepare you and your family for each of the disaster types to follow.

- ❑ 1 gallon of water/person/day
- ❑ Battery-powered or hand-crank radio (with extra batteries)
- ❑ Cell phone (with charger, inverter, or solar charger)
- ❑ Duct tape
- ❑ Dust mask
- ❑ First aid kit
- ❑ Garbage bags
- ❑ Local maps
- ❑ Manual can opener
- ❑ Moist towelettes
- ❑ Nonperishable food
- ❑ Plastic sheeting
- ❑ Weather radio (with extra batteries)
- ❑ Whistle (to signal for help)
- ❑ Wrench or pliers (to shut off utilities)

Additional Items to Consider:

- ❏ Additional clothing
- ❏ Baby needs (formula, diapers, etc.)
- ❏ Books, games, puzzles, or other forms of entertainment
- ❏ Cash
- ❏ Emergency reference material (first aid book, survival guide, etc.)
- ❏ Fire extinguisher
- ❏ Household bleach and a medicine dropper for purifying water (9 parts water to 1 part bleach)
- ❏ Important family documents
- ❏ Matches or lighters
- ❏ Paper cups, plates, and bowls, and plastic utensils
- ❏ Pencils or pens and paper
- ❏ Personal hygiene items
- ❏ Pet food and additional water
- ❏ Prescription medications and glasses
- ❏ Sleeping bags or blankets

EVACUATION BAG

- ❏ Cash
- ❏ Drinking water (an appropriate volume for the amount of time needed)
- ❏ Fire sticks or other easily ignited kindling material
- ❏ First aid kit
- ❏ Flashlight(s)
- ❏ Gloves
- ❏ GPS/maps
- ❏ Hat
- ❏ Identification (driver's license, passport, etc.)
- ❏ Insect repellent
- ❏ Matches and/or lighter
- ❏ Medications
- ❏ Metal pot for boiling water
- ❏ Nutritional food and snacks
- ❏ Rain coat/poncho
- ❏ Self-defense items (firearm, knife, pepper spray, stun gun)
- ❏ Sturdy bag or backpack (If you will be on foot, utilize an internal frame pack with load-distributing hip belt.)
- ❏ Sturdy footwear
- ❏ Sunblock

- [ ] Toiletries
- [ ] Utensils
- [ ] Water purification method (tablets, solutions, pumps, etc.)
- [ ] Weather-appropriate clothing (several days' worth)

FLOODS

Flooding is one of the most common, most costly, and most dangerous weather disasters that can occur. Both a light rain falling for several days and a deluge of water from the sky in a very short time frame can lead to deadly flood conditions. Our nation has seen massive devastation as a result of water overflowing or breaching its containment. It can be as large-scale as the Lake Pontchartrain levee breach during Hurricane Katrina in 2005 or your local stream pouring out of its banks, leaving roads impassable. Both can be extremely dangerous. Be prepared, stay alert, and be ready.

Preparation

- Identify local waterways that threaten your home, workplace, school, etc.
- Preplan multiple evacuation routes.
- Check with your insurance agent to confirm or obtain flood insurance.
- Prepare an evacuation bag or bags. Use the checklist on the previous page. The bag(s) should include personal hygiene items, water, snacks, spare cash, a flashlight, and anything else that you may need to keep your family safe for a minimum of 72 hours.
- Have a weather radio, smart phone app, or any other means to receive flood warnings and weather updates throughout the event.
- Make copies of important documents (birth certificates, passports, financial information, marriage certificates, etc.) and

keep them in a remote location such as a bank safe deposit box or at the very least with your evacuation supplies. Include your insurance agent's contact information.

- Take photographs of your possessions and store them on a removable memory device such as a flash drive or memory card. Keep it with the copies of your important documents.

Disaster Procedure

- Heed all appropriate flood warnings issued by the National Weather Service, local media, or any authority issuing instructions due to an impending flood.
- Move outdoor furniture or decorative items inside and important items to higher floors.
- Turn off water, gas, and electricity at the main shut-offs and unplug electrical equipment.
- Secure your home: Lock all doors and windows.
- Evacuate to a safe location using a predetermined route.
- Avoid walking or driving through moving water.
- Flood waters are usually toxic, filled with hazardous materials and dangerous bacteria. Avoid contact with it if at all possible.
- Beware of downed power lines that could go unnoticed on the ground, on a chain-link fence, or in water.
- Stay away from stray animals. They are likely to be afraid and defend themselves aggressively.

STORMS

Spring and summer months bring green grass, blooming flowers, and some of the strongest thunderstorms of the year. With them often come the potential for other threats such as tornados and flooding. With the storms come driving rain, dangerous winds, hail, and deadly lightning. On the average, lightning is attributed to approximately 50 deaths per year in the United States, making it one of the top storm-related killers.

While storms are a common-enough occurrence to not warrant much concern, they have the potential to be deadly and with every watch or warning should be given your attention.

Preparation

- Begin with the exterior. Remove dead or rotting trees located near your house that could fall and cause extensive damage.

- Make sure you are covered. Ensure your homeowner's insurance deductible and coverage meets your needs.

- Listen up. Keep a weather radio and stay tuned to forecasts, watches, and warnings. Understand the terminology. A thunderstorm watch means conditions are conducive to severe storms. A thunderstorm warning means that a storm is occurring or imminent and it poses a threat to life and property.

- Illuminate. It is common to lose power during storms. Be prepared with flashlights and spare batteries. While candles provide light, heat, and a calming ambiance, an open flame during stormy weather can be dangerous.

- Protect your electronics. Anything plugged into an electrical outlet is susceptible to damage from electrical surges due to a storm. Utilize a quality surge protector to give your computer, televisions, and appliances an extra measure of protection.

- Educate. Talk to your children about the dangers of storms. If the sky turns gray, it begins to rain, or they hear thunder, they should immediately come inside and stay there until the storm has safely passed.

- Have a safe place. Before the storm, identify a safe place in your home that is away from windows and not in danger of structural damage from large fallen trees.

- Check supplies. If you don't have a cache of supplies in a safe location in your home, assemble them before the storm so you will have access to your weather radio, flashlights, water, snacks, and other essential items.

Disaster Procedure

- Find a low area, such as a ravine, to avoid lightning, but be aware of the potential for flash flooding.

- Avoid natural lightning rods such as trees and hilltops.

- If you are in open water, get to shore immediately and seek shelter.

- If you are in a vehicle, locate a safe place to park and remain safely inside with the windows closed.

- If you feel your hair beginning to stand up (an indication that lightning is about to strike near you), make yourself as small as possible. Squat low to the ground with your head between your knees and hands over your ears rather than lying flat on the ground, which provides a larger surface for your body to conduct electricity.

- Stay in versus bug out. With enough advance warning you may have the opportunity to relocate ahead of the storm. Evaluate your options and, only if time allows, consider evacuating to a safer area.

- Reduce your chances of being shocked. During a storm it is best to avoid electrical equipment and plumbing. Both are prone to carrying electrical current from a lightning strike. Water also carries electrical current, which creates a deadly scenario if you are in the shower when lightning strikes your home.

- Avoid windows. Despite your curiosity as to what the storm looks like as it rages outside, avoid standing in front of windows or in doorways. Windows are easily broken by wind and storm-related projectiles. The shattered glass or windblown debris can cause serious injury.

- Remember your pets. Bring your pets inside and safely secure them with a leash, crate, or carrier. They could become frightened due to the weather and act out or run away.

BLIZZARDS

Extreme winter storms are as dangerous as any other weather-related phenomenon, but often, the real danger is not the storm itself, but the aftermath. With a blizzard comes extreme cold that lingers for days and often weeks after the storm. Many subsequent injuries and deaths are indirectly related to the storm. The accumulating snow causes homes to lose power and heat. People become trapped in their own homes and cannot reach or receive help. Traffic becomes paralyzed as the snow leaves roads too treacherous to pass. The conditions leave you trapped in place and left to fend for yourself, often without utilities or essential items needed for survival. Preparation is essential.

Preparation

- Back up your power. Assume you will lose power during a winter storm and have an alternative method ready to power some of your appliances. A backup generator and extra fuel are always a good idea. Remember to keep the generator outside as the gasoline engine can fill your home with deadly carbon monoxide.

- Check your supplies. Winter storm warnings lead to a rush of people procuring food and supplies. Grocery stores become crowded and essential food items can be sparse. Winter supplies such as windshield wiper fluid and ice melt disappear from shelves at a rapid rate. Prepare early before the storm to avoid fighting the crowds and taking the chance of doing without. Purchase a snow shovel. Have the means to clear a path in deep snow conditions. A snow blower is also useful, but may not function well in extremely deep snow.

- Avoid boredom. Entertainment items are often forgotten during disaster preparation. Place playing cards, board games, puzzles, or any variety of non-electronic entertainment with your supplies.

- Protect your pipes. Wrap exposed pipes in insulation and allow water to drip from faucets to avoid freezing. Disconnect exterior garden hoses from water spigots. This will decrease the chance of pipes freezing and breaking.

- Find your water shut-off. During extremely cold weather it is common for water pipes to freeze and break. Before the blizzard, locate your water shut-off so you will know how to stop the water if there were to be a pipe failure.

Disaster Procedure

- Monitor the weather. Stay informed of current and incoming weather. Winter storms can be extremely dangerous. With enough advance notice you can determine whether to shelter in place or evacuate.

- Stay put. If you have the option to avoid the snow altogether by staying inside during a storm, do so. Travel during winter storms can be treacherous. The wind and snow provide a dangerous combination that can easily lead to frostbite. The accumulating snow can also cover hidden dangers.

- Prioritize your heat. In the absence of power, heat becomes a precious commodity. Rather than trying to use supplemental heat for your entire house, focus on one or two rooms and try to keep them as insulated as possible, keeping doors closed and placing towels under doors and on window sills.

- Keep walking surfaces clear. Make attempts to keep your walkways and driveway clear. Remove the snow and use ice melt or kitty litter to help with traction. This allows for the ability to evacuate if needed and also creates access for emergency responders should the necessity arise.

- Recognize hypothermia. It is important to know the signs and symptoms of cold weather–related emergencies and what to do about them. See page 123 for specific details on how to recognize hypothermia and what to do about it.

- Check on your neighbors. Chances are you know your neighbors and have already identified individuals with special needs, including those with medical issues or who are very young or old. Once you have secured your home, check on your neighbors and help out where you can.

- Watch for hidden dangers. Accumulated snow can camouflage hazards hidden beneath. Ice, uneven terrain, and obstacles can be the least of your worries. Downed power lines are a common occurrence during a winter storm and can lay on the ground or across chain-link fences, energizing whatever they come in contact with.

- Do not leave your vehicle. If you are in your vehicle and caught in a winter storm, leaving your vehicle can be very dangerous. Instead, pull off the roadway if possible and turn on your hazard lights. If there is an occupied building nearby where you can seek shelter, consider relocating there. Otherwise, remain in your vehicle until help arrives.

EARTHQUAKES

An earthquake can be one of the most devastating disasters that can occur. Every state is at some risk for earthquakes and there is no "season" for them. They happen seemingly out of nowhere, although science has shown they are the result of tectonic plate movement, which cannot be predicted or stopped. Entire populations are caught completely off guard and are required to simply react. The devastation can be enormous. Preparation, safe procedures, and a little bit of luck will afford you the best possible outcome in an earthquake.

Preparation

- Create an emergency kit. It should contain food, water, clothing, and other essential supplies to sustain you and your family for a minimum of 72 hours.

- Secure heavy furniture. Large furniture such as cabinets and bookshelves should be secured to wall studs or masonry to avoid toppling during an earthquake. Never fasten it to Sheetrock. It is not strong enough to hold heavy objects in place.

- Store heavy objects low. Large or heavy objects should be placed on lower shelves to reduce the chance of them falling off and breaking or causing injury. Consider installing safety latches on cabinet doors.

- Install flexible pipe fittings. Fixed water and gas pipes easily break, creating a hazardous environment during an earthquake. Flexible fittings allow slight movement in the pipes. Consult a professional for installation.

- Identify safe places. In each room of your house, identify the safest place to take cover during an earthquake. Ideal places are under heavy furniture or against an interior wall away from windows or unsecured heavy furniture.

- Be ready at night. Keep a flashlight and sturdy shoes near each person's bed in case an earthquake occurs at night.

- Identify shut-offs. Know where your utility shut-offs are located and how to turn them off. If any tools are needed, keep them easily and quickly accessible.

Disaster Procedure

- Go to your safe place. Avoid exterior windows, doors, and walls. You should find a location near the interior of the home away from unsecured heavy furniture and light fixtures.

- Practice drop, cover, and hold on. Despite a popular theory, doorways are not the safest place to be during an earthquake. You should drop to your hands and knees, quickly crawl under heavy furniture, cover your head, and hold on.

- Stay in bed. If you are in bed, stay in bed. Cover your head with a pillow and wait for the tremors to stop. At night broken glass and debris will be difficult to see and avoid.

- Remain indoors. Do not go outside until the earthquake has completely stopped. If you are on an upper floor of a building with elevators, use the stairs to descend in case of aftershocks or a power outage.

- Expect alarms. Know in advance that building alarms will likely sound during an earthquake, even if there is no fire.

- Avoid power lines. If you are outside when the earthquake strikes, find a clear spot to get low and protect yourself, away from power lines, buildings, trees, and other hazards.

- Pull over. If you are in your vehicle at the time of the earthquake, pull safely over, being careful to avoid bridges, overpasses, tall buildings, and, if at all possible, power lines.

TORNADOS

Every year, particularly in the Midwest, spring thunderstorms generate a steady onslaught of tornados. Although every state is at some risk, "Tornado Alley," which is roughly the center of the country from top to bottom, receives the brunt. Funnel-shaped clouds descend from the sky to the ground and carve paths into the earth that are sometimes a mile wide. Winds reaching up to 300 mph cause mass destruction and numerous casualties. Most municipalities have tornado warning systems in place, but because of the tornado's nature, these systems often don't offer much advance notice. Preplanning before a tornado strikes can save you crucial minutes when the sirens are wailing and a storm is raging overhead.

Preparation

- Create an emergency kit. It should contain food, water, clothing, and other essential supplies to sustain you and your family for a minimum of 72 hours.

- Stay informed. Tune in to local news or a weather radio to stay informed of the status of approaching storms. This will help you determine if you are in the path, allow you time to prepare, and let you know when it is safe to resurface.

- Know the terminology. A "watch" means conditions are favorable for the development of a tornado. A "warning" means radar has identified cloud rotation in a storm cell or a tornado is already on the ground.

- Recognize the signs. Seek shelter immediately if you identify any of these signs: dark, often greenish clouds, a wall cloud, a cloud of debris, roaring noise, or a funnel cloud.

- Identify shelter. Know where you and your family can safely go when a tornado warning is given. It can be your basement, crawl space, or a small interior room on the lowest level.

- Expect high winds. Remove dead or decaying trees and shrubs near your house. Secure outside furniture and anything else that can become a projectile. Consider using mulch rather than rock for landscaping, due to it being less dangerous in a high-wind situation.

- Practice. Tornado drills are common in many schools. They should be common in your home as well. Ensure everyone in your family knows what to do and where to go.

Disaster Procedure

- Monitor the weather. If you fall under a tornado watch, stay aware of the status of the weather through local news, a weather radio, or smart phone apps. Ready your family and supplies in case conditions continue to deteriorate. If a tornado warning is issued, you and your family should seek immediate shelter, continue to monitor the weather for updates, and listen for an all-clear notification.

- Go to a safe place. Relocate to your predetermined safe location, which should be on the lowest level possible of the structure you are in. If there is no basement, go to an interior room with no windows, placing as many walls between you and the outside as possible. If you are in a mobile or manufactured home, go to the nearest sturdy building or storm shelter as soon as possible before the storm becomes imminent.

- Remember the pets. Most domestic pets can be put in a carrier or on a leash and brought to your safe place with you. Be sure to include pet supplies in your emergency kit. If you plan to relocate to a storm shelter, check beforehand to ensure that they allow pets. Most do not. For larger pets, prepare the emergency supplies and plan the measures to ensure their safety in advance.

- Stay in your car. If you are in your vehicle during a tornado, it is safest to remain in the vehicle. Drive to the nearest sturdy shelter. If debris begins to hit your vehicle before you reach the shelter, pull safely to the side of the road and park. Put on your seat belt and cover your head with your arms, a coat, or anything else you can use as protection from flying glass and debris.

- Get low. If you are outside during a tornado, there is no proven method to ensure your safety. The best-known approach is to find as low an area as possible, preferably a ditch or depression, and cover your body with anything you can find.

- Avoid the overpass. A common misconception is to locate a bridge or overpass to seek shelter. That is actually one of the most dangerous places you can be. Fierce tornadic wind currents are propelled under bridges and hurl flying debris through the area.

CIVIL UNREST

If you take a moment to stop and think about it, you are vulnerable in nearly every aspect of life. No matter how many layers of insulation and protection you provide yourself, certain levels of exposure remain. It could be in an airplane, in your office building, on the subway, or even in your own home. Attacks can come in many forms. Our civilization has seen explosive attacks, chemical attacks, radiological attacks, and even cyber attacks. They can come in the form of mass destruction in a major city or in the riots happening just outside your living room window. All of those areas should be considered in both preparation and procedure, but this section will specifically discuss civil unrest. As with any other disaster, what you do to prepare and how you respond when it happens will determine your level of loss.

Preparation

- Bolster your first aid kit. Demonstrations and riots often lead to violence. Make sure you have sufficient medical supplies to control bleeding, handle broken bones, and perform CPR. (Safely performing CPR requires a mask with a one-way valve to prevent fluid exposure.)

- Secure your doors and windows. Every door of your home should have multiple locking mechanisms. At least one of them should be a dead bolt. Every window should also have a lock. If someone wants to get into your house badly enough, there is no stopping them with locks, but the more security in place, the more it slows them down.

- Prepare personal security. During large-scale civil unrest, a home alarm system will offer little protection. Police simply cannot respond to every alarm; their hands will likely be full at the time. Many items can be used for personal self-defense: pepper spray, billy clubs, Tasers, etc. If you decide to keep a firearm, make sure to obtain a concealed weapons permit (if available in your state), stock up on ammunition, and practice shooting accuracy at a range.

- Consider internal security. Adding internal locks to important storage areas such as food pantries, a safe room inside your home, and a firearm cabinet will help deter would-be looters.

- Keep a cash stash. Often during civil chaos, banks and ATMs are not available. Having a stash of small bills in a safe and hidden location in your home will offer you the financial freedom to go several days without the need for a bank.

- Recruit your neighbors. Determine like-minded neighbors in advance. These are the people who could band together with you during civil unrest for protection and survival. Also note special needs individuals around you, such as the elderly or physically disabled. Have a plan in place to assist each other.

Disaster Procedure

- Stay informed. Local media will air immediate coverage of civil disturbances. Tune in and monitor their location and extent.

- Get out. If you have enough advance notice, evacuate the area. If time allows, take important documents, valuables, and keepsakes with you. But the most important thing is your safety. Get out and stay out until it is deemed safe to return.

- (Almost) barricade yourself in. If you do not have the opportunity to evacuate, barricade yourself in. Lock all points of entry and place heavy furniture in front of doors. Keep in mind, though, the possibility that you may need to evacuate during the disturbance. Allow yourself an opportunity to escape.

- Be ready. The most common dangers during civil unrest are physical violence, fire, and firearms. Locate an interior place in your home where you can remain low to the ground to avoid stray gunfire, and be ready to extinguish small fires. If there is anything larger than a small fire, get out immediately. As a visual reference, "small fires" are considered to be about the size of a trash can fire.

- Avoid public areas. Immediately evacuate to a safe place if you are in a public area, particularly a retail establishment that has any items that would be valuable to looters.

- Keep a level head and a low profile. Often, due to mob mentality, the initial target of the unrest becomes lost in the chaos. Suddenly everything and everyone are in danger. Maintain a clear head to keep yourself and your family safe. Stay out of the path, or at least the eyesight, of the rioters.

SUMMARY

Numerous other potential threats can affect you. Only you know what natural or man-made disasters are most likely to impact your way of life. It is extremely important for you to identify what those threats may be and take measures to prepare for and protect against them. There are extreme examples of elaborate underground shelters built in backyards. Fortunately, being prepared doesn't have to mean purchasing numerous supplies at exorbitant costs. Any measure of preparation will put you ahead of those who have subscribed to the "what are the chances" philosophy, playing the odds that "it" won't happen to them. Whether you invest your money or your time, you are investing in the safety of yourself, your family, and those around you.

CHAPTER 3
FIRE

Fire is a living, breathing thing and, when crackling in the fireplace, creates a tranquil and calming ambiance. It offers us the ability to warm ourselves and cook our food. In many ways, it provides the elemental foundation for some of the comforts we enjoy every day. At times, whether by accident or intent, it is allowed to freely burn without control, consuming oxygen and fuel at a frightening rate. The most common and immediate threat to human life and property, fire is capable of immense destruction and death that even professionals have difficulty suppressing. A basic understanding of fire will assist you when the need to build a fire arises. This understanding is vital to practice effective fire prevention.

THE SCIENCE OF FIRE

Fire is actually the result of a chemical reaction. For it to occur, four elements must be present. It is a delicate balance. If any one of the four are missing, fire cannot happen. In turn, by removing any one of the four elements, fire can be prevented or extinguished.

THE FOUR ELEMENTS OF FIRE

Heat: Heat can be supplied in a variety of ways: contact with a direct flame, friction, or mechanical generation, as with your vehicle's spark plugs, are a few examples. Once heat is generated, the energy transfers. It is transferred in one of three ways: direct contact, radiation, or convection.

- Direct contact is obviously when the source of the heat touches another object.

- Radiation is heat that is transferred through electromagnetic waves, such as when you put your hands near a campfire.

- Convection is the process of heat transfer from one location to the next by the movement of fluids. A common example of convection is a pot of boiling water on the stove. The surface of the bottom of the pot heats up the water, which rises, displacing the cooler water at the top.

Fuel: Fire fuel is basically any substance that is combustible. It can be solid (wood, fabric, natural fibers), liquid (gasoline, ethanol, kerosene), or gas (hydrogen, methane, butane). Interestingly, most solids and liquids do not actually burn. They are heated above their ignition temperature, which causes them to give off combustible vapors, a process known as pyrolysis. It is actually the escaping vapors during pyrolysis that burn. When a heat source comes in contact with fuel, the creation of fire begins.

Oxygen: Oxygen is crucial for fire to exist. There is approximately 21 percent oxygen in the air we breathe, which is enough to support combustion, but oxygen itself does not burn. The higher the concentration of oxygen in the air, the more intense the fire can burn. When you combine a heat source, fuel, and oxygen, only one more ingredient is needed to create fire.

Chemical reaction: A chemical reaction occurs when the exact mixtures of the other three components blend in the right concentrations to promote ignition.

By knowing the four parts necessary for fire, you can improve your fire prevention measures and understand your options when the need for fire extinguishment arises. By removing any one of the four components you will extinguish a fire. The most common method is to spray water or dispense a fire extinguisher, which cools a fire and removes the heat—fire extinguished. By shutting off the burner to your gas stove, you remove the fuel—fire extinguished. Putting the lid on a grease fire in a frying pan removes the oxygen—fire extinguished. There are a variety of ways to disrupt the chain reaction and eliminate fire. The key is prevention and early detection.

CLASSES OF FIRE

An understanding of fire should include the knowledge of how it is categorized. Fire is divided into classes by the type of fuel that is burning. In order to identify the type of extinguishing agent needed, a letter/symbol system was developed to differentiate the five categories. The classes of fire are:

CLASS OF FIRE	TYPE OF FIRE	PICTURE SYMBOL	EXTINGUISHER
A	Green triangle: ordinary combustibles such as wood, paper, and cloth		• Water • Foam spray • ABC powder • Wet chemical
B	Red square: flammable liquids		• Foam spray • ABC powder • Carbon dioxide
C	Blue circle: energized electrical equipment		• ABC powder
D	Yellow star: combustible metals		• ABC powder • Carbon dioxide
K	Black hexagon: cooking oils		• Wet chemical

Here's a simple way to remember the classes of fire:

- Class A leaves ash.
- Class B boils.
- Class C has a current.
- Class D is dense materials.
- Class K is for kitchen.

To effectively extinguish a fire, it is important to know what type of fuel is burning. Most portable fire extinguishers are capable of putting out multiple types. Commercial and residential extinguishers primarily suppress Class A, B, and C fires. Class A and B are often given a numerical value (1A to 40A and 1B to 640B) depending on the amount of extinguishing agent required. The higher the number, the greater the amount called for. Class D and K extinguishers are more specialized and less common. The type of fire or fires that can be put out by a particular extinguisher should be clearly visible on the label. If you are not sure, the safest thing to do would be to evacuate the area.

SIZE-UP CONSIDERATIONS

As previously discussed, in a fire situation, it is essential that you conduct a quick but thorough size-up. Remember, a size-up is no more than quickly processing as much accurate and relevant information as you can in order to develop a plan of action. A rapid size-up will help you determine what you will do in a situation involving fire. Because of the obvious urgency of a fire, critical decisions are often needed right away based on effectiveness and safety. Your own personal safety is the top consideration, followed by the life safety of others.

A former battalion chief with my fire department would always say that when he shows up on a scene, he wants to know three things about the fire: Where has it been? Where is it now? Where is it going? That was his simplified way of sizing up a fire. By knowing where the fire has been you may be able to infer what caused it and what kind of damage there may be prior to your arrival. Though this may be guesswork, it is vital information when you are evaluating the situation and putting the safety of yourself and other rescuers at risk. Where it is now will give you a snapshot of what your realistic opportunity is to extinguish the fire. If it is a small fire that can be put out safely with a fire extinguisher, then you may elect to take an offensive posture and put out the fire. If it is larger and you are not sure if you can safely extinguish it, your response may be to evacuate. Finally, where it is going gives you the opportunity to predict what is in immediate danger, whether your efforts will be effective, or if evacuation is the best course of action.

WHAT TO DO

If it is a small fire, roughly the size of a trash can fire, you can attempt to extinguish it as long as a few criteria are met:

1. It is a small fire; one that can be put out by a fire extinguisher.

2. You have activated the fire alarm and/or called 911.

3. You have a partner. Always avoid fighting a fire alone.

4. You can fight the fire and escape safely.

5. You approach the fire cautiously and back safely away. Never turn your back on a fire, even one that you believe to be extinguished.

PORTABLE FIRE EXTINGUISHERS

You pass portable fire extinguishers every day. They are required in businesses, churches, schools, and anywhere else people gather. Even though they are so common that they go unnoticed most of the time, you've probably given little thought to their operation. When the need arises for a fire extinguisher to be used, safe and effective operation can make a considerable difference. Learning to use one should not happen when the fire is burning in front of you. Operating a fire extinguisher is not a difficult task, but there are basic information and skills that you should know.

More than likely you have one in your home and several at work. Pick one up and look at it. You will notice a few things. First of all, there will be a label on it from Underwriters Laboratories or a similar organization. That label tells you that the product was tested in accordance with specific procedures and that it passed. You will also see a rating, based on extinguishing agent, of what types of fires can be put out with that particular extinguisher.

The most common type of portable fire extinguishers is multipurpose, dry chemical, ABC extinguishers. They are small, easy to operate, and extinguish the majority of fires types that you may come across. They will have 10 to 20 seconds of discharge with a range of 8 to 12 feet. You should be effective with your placement so as not to waste vital product.

When using a fire extinguisher, you should be able to say yes to the following questions:

1. If you attempt to extinguish the fire, are there two ways away from the fire?

2. Do you have the correct extinguisher for the type of fuel burning?

3. Is the extinguisher capable of putting out the size of fire you are facing?

4. Is the area free from other hazards?

5. Can you put out the fire in five seconds or less?

If the answer to any of the above questions is no, you should leave the building immediately and shut all doors on your way out to help contain the fire.

There are four major components to a portable fire extinguisher: A cylinder, a carrying handle with trigger, a hose, and a pressure gauge. Hold the extinguisher upright and utilize the following PASS acronym to follow the steps of fire extinguisher operation:

Pull the pin out of the extinguisher handle.

Aim directly at the fire.

Squeeze the handle.

Sweep back and forth at the base of the fire.

Pull the pin from the handle. The pin serves as a safety device and prevents you from activating the extinguisher. Aim the nozzle at the base of the fire. The temptation will be to aim at the flames. Your extinguishing agent will go right through them, so be sure to focus your nozzle toward the base of the fire at the fuel. Begin from a safe distance away. Squeeze the trigger and sweep back and forth, moving slowly closer to the fire until it is out. Slowly back away from the fire. Remember to always face the fire, even when backing out of the room.

FIRE SUPPRESSION SAFETY RULES

Work in teams. Working in groups of two or three helps to ensure safety, with more eyes available to spot hazards or changing conditions.

Have a backup team. A backup team isn't always an option. There may not be enough people to allow one, but when there is, you should consider having a team ready. If your suppression efforts fail, a backup team will be available to offer support.

Use safety equipment. Glasses, gloves, and a helmet, among other things, should all be used if available. If you do not have proper safety equipment, you should leave the building immediately.

Have two ways out. Always have two ways out of the fire area. Fires are unpredictable and often spread quickly. Your exit may become blocked. Having a second way out should always be a part of your plan.

Observe smoke conditions and avoid smoke-filled areas. More turbulent smoke means more dangerous fire conditions. If smoke is pushing out of the top of the door, do not enter. Also, if you notice than an area contains a significant amount of smoke, there are likely dangers present that exceed your level of training and equipment.

Check doors for heat. Feel a closed door with the back of your hand. Working from the bottom of the door up, use the back of your hand to feel the door for heat. If the door is hot, do not open it. If you do, you risk being burned as well as adding oxygen to the fire.

Stay low. Smoke and heated gases rise. Squat below the dangerous air.

Keep a safe distance. Remember that an extinguisher's reach is 8 to 12 feet. Do not get closer than necessary.

Do not fight large fires. Fighting fires is best left to the professionals, but when they are not available and you are faced with a fire, use caution. A general rule of thumb is that if a fire is bigger than you are, it is too big for you to safely put out.

Face the fire. Never turn your back on a fire. Conditions can change without warning and you should be aware of what is happening.

Overhaul. Make sure the fire is extinguished and stays extinguished. With a tool, move around the charred material to ensure there aren't hidden embers that could return to a free-burning fire.

HAZARDOUS MATERIALS

Hazardous materials are stored and transported all around us every day. As long as they are encapsulated in their respective containers, they are relatively safe. When they escape or the containers are compromised, the dangers can be catastrophic. Without proper training, there are a very limited number of things you can do when handling hazardous materials, if anything at all. The most important thing you can do is to recognize hazardous materials and avoid them.

There are clues to help you identify locations where hazardous materials may be stored or in transit.

Type of occupancy. Some occupancies are inherently prone to have hazardous materials on site. Industrial plants, manufacturing facilities, construction sites, and even vehicle repair shops are all examples of occupancies that typically have numerous hazardous materials stored on the premises. One of the least considered and most common locations that contains hazardous materials is a residential garage. People are notorious for storing gas cans, pesticides, and random chemicals there. Any type of occupancy that may contain hazardous materials should require extra caution when you are conducting your size-up and establishing your plan of action.

Placards. A placard is a diamond-shaped notice signifying the presence of a hazardous material. The United States Department of Transportation requires placards on containers that hold hazardous materials when they are being shipped in the United States, Canada, and Mexico. Hazardous materials placards will contain specific information regarding the material and an ID number correlating to the specific chemical information regarding it. Another type of placard known as a NFPA 704 Diamond is commonly seen in commercial occupancies. It has four quadrants that each signify a hazard and a corresponding number that ranges from 1 to 4. The higher the number, the higher the risk. The red quadrant describes a material's flammability. The blue quadrant indicates the health hazard. The yellow quadrant states the reactivity. The white quadrant indicates "other" hazards. Know that placards do not apply to small quantities, so just because you don't see a placard does not necessarily mean that a hazardous material isn't present. The most important thing to know about placarding is that it should be considered a STOP sign. If you see a placard of any kind, you should evacuate uphill and upwind.

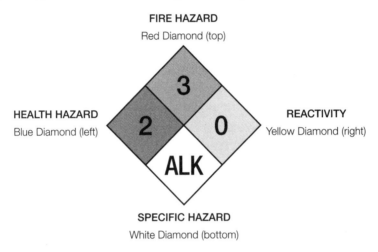

Sights, sounds, and smells. Using your senses to discover a hazardous material leak is a last resort. If you see a spill of any kind, you should evacuate. If you hear the hissing of a gas leak, you should evacuate. If you smell natural gas or a strong chemical odor, you should evacuate. Hazardous materials can be extremely dangerous in very small quantities and should be avoided at all costs.

Be aware of the presence of hazardous materials, whether there is a placard in place or not. If there is a placard of any kind, treat it as a stop sign and evacuate the area. And if you evacuate due to a hazardous materials leak, remember to withdraw uphill and upwind.

FIRE PREVENTION IN THE HOME

Although the number of injuries and deaths in residential fires have decreased, the fires are more dangerous than ever. Home furnishings used to be made of natural fibers like wood and cotton. In recent years a transition has occurred. Now, nearly everything in your home is made of synthetic fibers and other petroleum-based products. That means that because the "fuel" in your home is primarily made from oil, fires can burn very quickly and will be extremely hot.

Fire-prevention measures should be taken far in advance of a disaster. They should be established early and practiced often. During an extreme weather event or civil disturbance, the threat of fire greatly increases.

Education is your best defense against the danger of fire. Knowledge will allow you to engage in good fire prevention practices as well as know what to do if a fire occurs. It begins with some of the basics that we were all taught as children and pass on to our own children. The rules haven't changed.

Update your safety equipment. Several fire safety items should be considered critical. Your home should have working smoke alarms on every floor of your house, preferably every room. Change the batteries twice a year (often in the spring and fall). When the clocks are changed, the batteries should be too. Have a fire extinguisher placed prominently in your home where it can be easily found. Consideration should be given to having a fire extinguisher on each floor. At least one carbon monoxide (CO) detector, located where it can wake you up at night, should be in place. The best option for a CO detector is a plug-in model with a battery backup and an LED screen that will inform you of the exact level of carbon monoxide in your house.

Check electrical equipment. Electrical equipment should be checked for loose, frayed, or faulty wiring. Any issues with electrical wiring require immediate attention and discontinued power. Also, be careful not to overload electrical outlets. Sometimes called the "electrical octopus," standard wall outlets can be overloaded with adaptors and extension cords, which will create a dangerous fire hazard.

HOME FIRE SAFETY CHECKLIST

❑ Keep all matches and lighters away from children.

❑ Check electrical appliances for loose or frayed cords.

❑ Ensure there are no electrical cords under rugs or carpet.

❑ Avoid overloaded outlets, known as the "electrical octopus."

❑ Install GFCI (ground fault circuit interrupter) outlets near water sources, such as the kitchen and bathrooms.

❑ Lamps and fixtures should not be in contact with any fabric.

❑ Have your furnace inspected by a licensed professional annually.

❑ Keep space heaters away from flammable items, such as curtains, reading material, and bedsheets.

❑ Have your fireplace cleaned and inspected annually.

❑ Equip your fireplace with a metal fire screen or heat-tempered glass doors.

SAFETY EQUIPMENT

❑ Install smoke alarms on every level of the home and in sleeping areas.

❑ Keep smoke alarms in working order and change the batteries twice a year.

❑ Replace smoke alarms every 10 years.

❑ Install a carbon monoxide alarm on every level of the home or, at a minimum, near each sleeping area.

❑ Have at least one working fire extinguisher in the home.

❑ Keep emergency fire safety ladders in bedrooms above the ground floor.

HOME ESCAPE PLAN

❑ Identify two ways out of each room (including basement rooms).

❑ Come up with an escape plan and practice it with the entire family.

❑ Ensure everyone knows the rule: "Get out and stay out."

❑ Select a family meeting place.

Separate heat sources and fuel. Combustibles such as magazines and newspapers, fabric, and furniture should be kept at a distance from heat sources, and flammable liquids should be in protected, approved containers. Also, keep lighters and matches in a secure place out of reach of children. These are all good practices that keep heat sources away from fuel.

Call 911. If there is any kind of fire incident in your home, always call 911. Even the smallest fires can quickly become raging infernos. Burning embers from a small fire can find their way into places that you can't see and wreak havoc. It is not uncommon for a small trash can fire or cooking fire to sneak even the tiniest of embers inside of your wall that, given time, will create a large hidden fire. Most fire departments carry with them thermal imaging cameras that allow them to detect temperature differences within objects and walls. They can tell if a small fire is hiding in your wall without having to tear it out to check. In an extreme weather event or disaster type of situation, a fire department response may not happen in a timely fashion, but you should make the call anyway. At least let them know you had an incident and they will respond as quickly as they can given the circumstances.

Have an escape plan. Your workplace is likely required by municipal code to not only have a fire escape plan in place, but also to post the plan where everyone can see it and practice the plan. It is vitally important to have a fire escape plan at home as well. From every room in the house, there should be two ways out and everyone in the home should know those options. In most cases it is a door and a window. If the window is the second way out of a particular room, consider purchasing a fire escape safety ladder. They fold down and can be tucked neatly under a bed.

Select a meeting place. The meeting place for your family should be a spot located outside the home, in a safe area, that can be accessed by family members of all ages. Many people have chosen a front yard tree or the mailbox by the street. Both are good locations. Ideally your safe place, such as a neighbor's porch, will protect you from the elements. If you are in a multi-family building, consider a safe place in close proximity to your building. Choose your location carefully and ensure that all family members know where to find it.

Practice. An escape plan and an established meeting place are only beneficial if everyone knows them. Once you have evaluated your options and decided on a plan and where to meet, you must practice. Walk through it a few times and discuss what went well and what went badly. Make changes that are necessary and make a point to practice and reevaluate often.

SUMMARY

Understanding fire gives you an advantage when trying to contain it, beginning with the ability to recognize and reduce the risk. Statistics show that when you practice good fire prevention by readying your home with the proper alarms and extinguishers, your risk of injury by fire is reduced significantly. Include your entire family in fire safety talks and practices. Even children should be taught the family fire safety plan and what is expected of them.

Fire can be tricky business following a disaster. The potential is virtually everywhere that has been affected and fires are often being "fed" by utilities. Natural gas and electrical lines become compromised and are no longer safely contained. They can cause fire ignition and continue to supply virtually limitless fuel to a fire. Be aware of this when deciding your action plan. When you encounter fire, a risk assessment is critical. The first thing you must do is evaluate the size of the fire against what you hope to accomplish, be it extinguishment or a rescue. There is no benefit in putting yourself and others at risk to try to save what is already lost. There is one philosophy that says if you put out the fire, a lot of the other associated problems, such as destruction and life safety issues, go away. If you deem it safe and appropriate to try to extinguish the fire, use safe practices and put that fire out.

CHAPTER 4
LIGHT SEARCH
AND RESCUE

Few situations are more frightening, stressful, or critical than when a life or multiple lives are in danger and you have the opportunity to make a difference. You instinctively rush to help. Unfortunately, the goodwill of civilian helpers often leads to additional injuries and even deaths. Untrained volunteers with the best of intentions flock to the aftermath of major disasters, only to compound the problems. These unprepared survivors often cannot adequately evaluate the scenario during a spontaneous rescue effort. They simply *help*.

In the aftermath of a disaster, there is the potential for rescue all around. In order to avoid making a bad thing worse, you must make your personal safety and the safety of other rescuers your primary concern.

Then, you may have to make an unfortunate risk assessment: risk a lot to save a lot versus risk little to save little. You have to make major decisions based on very little information, forging a plan of action based on what your brain is taking in and processing combined with assumptions you have to make from what you see and hear.

The most import actions you can take prior to a rescue are to evaluate your risk, ensuring that you have adequate training and capabilities, and then doing the most good for the greatest number of people. The key steps to construct a successful search-and-rescue operation are: size up, search/locate, and rescue.

Search-and-rescue procedures can actually be identified *before* the disaster. You can, and should, assess what resources you have available to you. Search-and-rescue resources include things such as personnel, equipment, and tools. Preplan your rescue efforts by asking yourself a few questions:

Personnel

- Who lives or works in your area?
- Do any of them have a special skill that could be an advantage during a disaster?
- Do any of them require special needs?
- What hours will they likely be available to you? What hours will they not be available?
- What would be the best way to contact them or mobilize?

Equipment

- What equipment would be available to you?
- Where is it located?
- Who knows how to operate it?
- How do you access it?
- In what types of scenarios would it be beneficial?

Tools

- What tools are available to you?
- Are any special skills needed to operate them? If so, who could do so?
- Are there enough tools available to lift, move, or cut disaster debris?
- Do you have access to those tools?

SIZE-UP

As a potential rescuer, sizing up a disaster situation can be one of the most difficult circumstances you find yourself in. Not only are you still processing the events that just altered your world, now you must make critical choices in a very short time frame. It is more important than ever to do a thorough but rapid size-up. You are going to have to determine if those in danger can self-rescue or if they need help.

I have often found that when a person is placed in a dangerous situation, given an opportunity, they will self-rescue. The preservation of one's own life is instinctive and causes us to act sometimes without conscious thought. When someone unexpectedly falls into water they don't assess the situation to determine the best response. They immediate recognize that they cannot breathe and spontaneously move to get to air. The head angles up, straightening the airway, and arms and legs kick, propelling the body toward the surface of the water. It is a reflex of survival—the body's resolve to ensure its own continuity. The same response applies in a disaster situation. If there is present danger, people will remove themselves if at all possible.

In scenarios where the danger cannot be removed and one cannot rescue themselves, action is required. Life safety is the number one incident priority. With that in mind you must determine if it is safe for you to act, remembering that if you become injured or trapped yourself, you only compound the problem.

Assuming that there is no opportunity for immediate help from emergency responders, you must begin a more thorough evaluation of the situation if you are considering taking action. The first thing that must be done is to gather the facts. What has happened? What is happening now? What is likely going to happen next?

Prediction and probability are part of your size-up. You can't possibly predict the future, but because you will be working in a dangerous situation, it is critically important that you consider what may or may not happen next. "What if?" is one of the most important questions you can ask to minimize the danger to yourself and other rescuers. You won't have a lot of time to obtain all of the information you will likely want, so plan for a worst-case scenario.

DAMAGE ASSESSMENT

After determining what has happened and predicting what is to come, you will evaluate the extent of the damage. Be aware of three damage levels: light, moderate, and heavy. The amount of damage will determine what actions, if any, you should consider. Specific visual cues can help you assess the amount of damage and whether or not it is safe to proceed.

A good assessment of the building will not come from a singular view. Walk a complete lap around it, observing from all sides. Occasionally, the size of the building or other factors will prevent you from "walking a lap." In those situations, simply make the best decision based on everything you are able to observe. Look up, down, left, and right. Take in the overall picture. Make special note of dangerous conditions, such as downed power lines, fallen trees, cracked walls, and other perils that could present problems for

Light damage

a search-and-rescue operation. Also, note general layout and landscaping concerns, such as rock walls or in-ground swimming pools that could pose a threat to rescuers.

Light damage. Superficial damage is considered light. Cosmetic cracks in walls and broken windows are indicative of minor issues that should not deter you from entering a structure. Light damage is slight enough that rescue actions can and should be taken. Unless you see more substantial destruction, no evidence signifies that a collapse is likely. Interior contents can give the illusion that extensive damage has occurred when in actuality it has not. Toppled furniture, empty bookshelves, and broken dishes give the impression of large-scale destruction, but should be considered trivial in the big picture. If light damage is confirmed, you can proceed with caution. YOUR GOAL: Locate, conduct triage, and remove victims based on medical priority.

Moderate damage. Visible evidence of structural damage is initially a stop sign for you. Large cracks in a building's foundation as well as numerous wall cracks can indicate bigger problems. Use extreme caution if you opt to enter a building with moderate damage. Also, evaluate the interior for structural damage. Occasionally, structures with moderate damage will be associated with fires or gas leaks, as well as creaking or groaning. In that case, the best action you can take is to secure the perimeter and warn others of the dangers you have identified. The building must be considered unstable and should not be entered. YOUR GOAL: Locate, stabilize, and immediately remove victims to a safe area while keeping the number of rescuers inside the structure to a minimum.

Heavy damage. One of the easiest levels of damage to identify is heavy damage. A structure that has any obvious signs of instability, such as leaning, partial collapse, or removal from the foundation altogether should not be entered under any circumstances. Do not attempt to access a building that has completely collapsed. The potential for hidden dangers is too vast for you to do so safely. Never enter a structure that has sustained heavy damage. YOUR GOAL: From outside the structure, locate

Moderate damage

Heavy damage

victims by voice and secure the perimeter by controlling access into the building with untrained volunteers.

When there is heavy structural damage to a building, be aware of the possibility of a full collapse. The "collapse zone" of a building is an area around a building equal to one-and-a-half times its height. Buildings that are more than a few stories tall will have large collapse zones that may not be feasible to avoid. When you approach a building that shows signs of heavy damage, approach it from a corner if possible. The corners of a building provide the safest area within the collapse zone if the building were to topple. Be aware of the collapse potential and, if you must work in the collapse zone, do it as quickly as possible and then relocate to a safer area.

SEARCH
GO VS. NO GO

When a rescue is required, there is going to come a point when you have to make a go or no-go determination. It can be one of the most difficult decisions you will ever face. The hardest part will be adequately evaluating the situation rather than emotionally reacting. Ideally, you would have the time to consider the weather, the damage, the risk, your training, the tools needed, and whether or not you have all the people you need to safely conduct the rescue. Rarely will you have the time to address all of those factors adequately. You are going to have to make the decision with as much information as you can get as quickly as possible.

Part of your fact-gathering should include key topics: time and occupancy, weather, resources, and hazards. Fire departments do this all the time. They are called to a fire and, due to what they see when they arrive, make critical decisions based on probabilities and what little information they can quickly obtain.

Time and occupancy. Does the time of day or night lend itself to there being occupants in the building? Depending on the structure type, you can make certain assumptions based on the time. A school during a weekday in the fall is going to be heavily occupied. That same school at midnight or in the middle of the summer will have far less of an occupancy hazard.

Although there are no guarantees, you will have to make decisions based on what little information you have. Take note of the time. Who would likely be there at that hour of day or night? Are cars in the driveway or parking lot? Is there anyone around who would be a credible source to tell you if anyone is in the structure? Is there anyone inside the structure with special needs or who requires special considerations? Most of this information will be based on your best guess.

Weather. Weather will often hamper a rescue and put you at an even greater risk. Quickly evaluate whether the conditions are getting worse, staying the same, or improving, and how they will affect you and your rescue.

Resources. Do you have the resources needed to perform the rescue? You may simply need to gather more people to help get the job done, or find this is a complex or technical rescue requiring trained professionals. This should be determined before rescue is attempted. It can be unnecessarily dangerous to put fellow rescuers in harm's way without the appropriate resources needed to perform their task. Consider keeping tools that may help you conduct a rescue in your disaster preparations, such as flashlights, gloves, and rope.

Hazards. Depending on a building's occupancy, you can expect certain hazards. Are there dangers that may be threatening to rescuers such as indoor pools, hazardous materials, high-voltage electricity, or other onsite factors? There are inherent risks associated with specific kinds of buildings or businesses. Look for clues such as signs or hazardous materials placards to help identify onsite hazards.

If any indicators reveal that it is not safe for you to perform a rescue, you should consider it a *no-go* situation. A lot of good can be done safely from outside of the structure. By putting yourself in harm's way, you run the risk of becoming another casualty.

As the company officer in the fire department, part of my job is to evaluate a scene. One of the most challenging decisions that I have to make at a fire is determining whether there is the potential for rescue or if the event has deteriorated enough that the situation is not survivable. When my fire truck arrives and there is heavy fire in a bedroom where a victim may be, I have to quickly determine if the situation is survivable and worth risking the lives of the firefighters I send in to perform the rescue. Is it realistically an environment where life is sustainable? I have to risk a lot to save a known life, but I also have an obligation to help ensure that the men and women on my crew will return safely to their families at the end of their shift and not be injured or killed trying to save what was already lost.

At one particular fire, we arrived at the house to find heavy fire engulfing the majority of the second floor and much of the first. The fire occurred during the early morning hours when people are typically waking up for work or school. We received information that an invalid resided in the home and had not been seen that morning. The decision was made to attempt a rescue. One company made entry into the second-floor bedroom window where the victim was believed to be. I assigned my company to fight our way to the stairs to protect the possible egress for the rescuers. Fire was on all sides of us. We inched our way forward, trying to get into a position that would allow us to be able to protect the other crew and the victim. As we were making our way to the stairwell, the ceiling and roof structure began to collapse around us. We were forced to back out, as was the rescue crew. We found out later that there had been no one home. The family was on vacation. In hindsight, there was no possible way that a victim could have survived, had there been one in that bedroom. It was, at best, a futile effort. Our failure to recognize the reality of the situation put two crews at risk of losing their lives for a person that wasn't there and property that was already beyond saving. I have the responsibility to make decisions based on life safety: for victims at a fire and the safe return of the men and women on my crew.

You too have an obligation to be there for your family after the disaster recovery. When you consider a rescue, you owe it to yourself, your family, and those assisting you to determine if you are facing a rescue or a recovery.

INITIATING A SEARCH

Even if you determine that it is not safe to enter a structure, you can still locate victims and perform a rescue from the exterior. While safely outside, look in doors and windows. You may be able to recognize injured or trapped victims. Let them know that it is safe to come out and that they should do so as quickly and safely as possible, being aware of the debris and dangers around them. If you don't see anyone, call out. Disoriented or trapped victims, or even people who had entered seeking shelter, may remain silently in the building. It is common for people to seek shelter and have no way of knowing when it is safe to come out. Your calling out to them may be the catalyst they need to simply come out. Have those who are able to exit the building on their own. Whether they are still sheltered in their chosen safe place or "walking wounded," you can coach them out of the structure without placing yourself in danger. They will also be a good resource to find out if there is anyone else in the building.

In the situations where the structure is stable enough to enter, follow the guidelines and methods to conducting a successful interior search. The first, which should always be done, is to ensure that all available safety equipment is being used. At the very least, one should wear a helmet, gloves, and safety glasses. Protecting your head, eyes, and hands will allow you to function safely in most structurally sound buildings. Other preferences would be to wear long sleeves, long pants, and sturdy work boots. Often, following a disaster, one of the most dangerous aspects of a search is the dust entering your lungs. Particularly if there has been any kind of collapse, dust will be both an irritant as well as a potentially deadly pathogen. Rescuers should wear a mask or respirator if at all possible. N95 masks (cloth masks with elastic straps, which filter dust and some airborne diseases) are common, easily stored in your preparation supplies, and very effective at blocking particulates from entering your lungs. Wear ALL available safety equipment.

Next, work in teams of at least two people. This concept is taught to emergency responders at all levels. Using the "buddy system" has proven to be a safe and preferred method for the rescuers and has contributed to more successful search-and-rescue operations. By working in teams, you double your chance to see or hear someone. You also have extra help to remove someone who is trapped or offering assistance if you become lost or trapped yourself.

Hazards are literally all around you. You must always be alert for sharp objects, hazardous materials, signs of fire, electrical dangers, natural gas leaks, uneven or missing floor space, and overhead objects that could fall or collapse. Always reevaluate what you are doing and if it is safe to continue, keeping in mind that the two most frequent reasons for rescuer fatalities are disorientation and secondary collapse. A secondary collapse is an event that occurs after the initial one, when damage weakens the structure and, at some point during or after rescue operations, it collapses. If, at any time, the situation changes or you discover significant dangers, abort your rescue and safely evacuate the building.

WHERE TO LOOK

After a size-up has been performed, the walking wounded evacuated, and a search determined necessary, the first step in initiating a search is to interview bystanders who may be familiar with specific knowledge of the structure and the whereabouts of those who may still be inside. They are your greatest source of information. You will want to know specifics and have to ask the right questions. Often, after a disastrous event, those affected may be shell-shocked. They may be confused and unable to formulate a singular thought. It is common for someone in that state to either exaggerate information or offer an inaccurate report. It isn't intentional, but a byproduct of what just occurred. Keeping that in mind, you will still want to gather as much information from them as you can.

- Is there anyone inside?
- Who are they and where would they be right now?
- Where are the shelters in the building and the common exit routes?
- What will be the quickest and safest route to get to the exit routes?

Disaster survivors are often found in the void spaces of a building. During a particularly strong thunderstorm, my engine company responded to the partial collapse of a house. A mother and her young daughter were found alive in the void space created by a collapsed wall. In this case, they were attempting to seek shelter when part of the roof and an interior wall came down on them. Fortunately for them, the interior wall fell over and came to rest against an exterior wall, creating the void space where they ended up. The collapsed wall ended up sheltering them from other falling debris. This isn't always the case, but for that mother and daughter, the void space provided an accidental and lucky safe haven.

Common household voids where people are located are bathtubs, closets, and under furniture. They either seek shelter there before the event or end up identifying it as a safe place afterward. When searching a home, consider the void spaces where survivors may be hidden. Oftentimes those void spaces offer the best chance for survival when the structure is collapsing around them.

When a building collapses it rarely falls flatly and evenly. Walls give out and ceilings or upper floors collapse, creating structural voids. These voids are spaces in which victims may have been trapped or sought protection. Three types of structural voids are identified in a collapse. Each is named by the void that it creates:

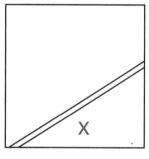 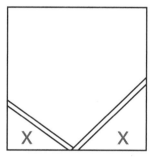 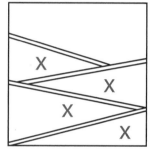

Lean-to void. A lean-to void is created when a collapsed wall is leaning against an upright wall, creating a pocket of space.

V void. A V void happens when the middle of an upper floor or ceiling collapses and the ends lean against outside walls.

Pancake void. A pancake void occurs when multiple floors collapse onto each other and offer very little, if any, survivable void spaces. They are the most difficult and time-consuming to search.

TIP: Shut off gas before you enter a damaged structure. Shut off the electricity at the panel as you make your way through.

EXTERIOR SEARCH PROCEDURES

Occasionally, searches are conducted in an open area. This is typically done with many volunteers. To effectively search an open area, the entire group must work systematically and follow the search procedures set forth by those in charge of the operation.

Whoever is in charge should first set up a grid of the area. Documentation is important to ensure that the entire area is searched and nothing is missed. Distances between rescuers should be set according to the number of participants, visibility, and the terrain. Search in straight lines if possible, documenting the entire process. Utilize overlapping patterns to ensure full coverage of the area.

Lay out buildings in the search area in the A, B, C, D method. Side A is the front, or the "address" side. Then, going left around the building, B is the side, C is the back, and D is the other side. Everyone who is assisting with the search should be aware of the terminology and be able to advise if they are on side A, B, C, or D.

If the search is going to be a long endeavor, consider the needs of rescuers who will be volunteering. Will lighting be needed? Food? Water? Tools? Part of the rescue operation should be ensuring that rescuers have what is needed to perform their task. Prepare backup teams to be ready to replace the existing team or teams. This helps ensure that if something were to happen to the initial people performing a search, there is a backup crew ready to help. Rotating people also reduces fatigue. While waiting, backup teams should drink plenty of water, eat enough food to maintain their strength through their operational period, discuss what the current teams are doing, and determine what is working and what could be done better. The backup teams should identify what has been searched and what the goals are for the next team to avoid redundancy.

> **TIP:** While performing a search, stop frequently to listen for voices, tapping, movement, or other noises created by victims.

INTERIOR SEARCH PROCEDURES

When an interior search is required, the more assistance you can get, the more successful the operation will be. When victims are trapped it is easy for people to respond emotionally and rush to help without giving thought to overall safety. It can be difficult to gather everyone who wants to assist. They are often focused on rescue. Every effort should be made to assemble all the volunteers and coordinate the search. If there is an authority present, they will brief the searchers as to what to look for and how to best conduct the search. If there is no authority present, one person should be selected as the team leader or incident commander. That person will coordinate the searchers and the overall plan.

Effective search procedures will be systematic and thorough, avoid unnecessary duplication, and document the results of the search.

Search Markings

During a large-scale disaster, professional search-and-rescue teams use a common marking system to avoid duplication of their efforts. If a structure has been searched there will be markings known as "x codes" near the front door (or as close as they can get to what is left of the door) to inform other volunteer rescuers or professional search-and-rescue personnel that a particular building has been searched and what was and is currently inside. It is not recommended to mark the door itself or the wall that is covered by the swinging door in case the markings are not easily visible. A variety of options may be used when marking a search area. Spray paint is common, but can be sloppy. Large permanent markers or a lumber marker/crayon are other options. Whatever you choose, you will want it to be as "permanent" as possible.

As you enter a search area, make a single slash (half of what will eventually become a large "x"). If you have it available, you can use duct tape for your search "x" slashes. Write your name, agency, or group ID at the nine o'clock position. Then write the date and time in the 12 o'clock position. Leave room to document your "time out" when you are done with your search.

Upon exiting a search area, make another slash (completing the "x"). Write the time you leave in the upper quadrant under your "time in." In the right, or three o'clock position, write the areas of the structure that were searched and any specific information about hazards. The lower, six o'clock quadrant, is where you will enter information about the victims located in the search area. Write "L," for living victims, and then the number found. You can also include "D," for deceased victims, and the number found. You may also include where the victims were taken. For example, a local shelter or hospital.

These markings give other rescuers a quick confirmation that the area has been searched and communication about what was found and done. Off to the side of the "x," you will occasionally see other information such as "gas shut off" or "pets inside," The information noted on your x-code also offers concerned friends and family members crucial clues about their loved ones.

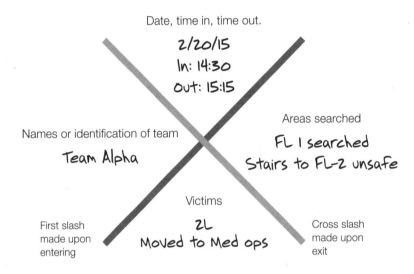

Date, time in, time out.

2/20/15
In: 14:30
Out: 15:15

Names or identification of team

Team Alpha

Areas searched

FL 1 searched
Stairs to FL-2 unsafe

Victims

2L
Moved to Med ops

First slash made upon entering

Cross slash made upon exit

Conducting an Interior Search

To ensure that all areas of a building have been searched, professional search-and-rescue personnel use a systematic search pattern. You can choose what systematic approach works for you, but the most common is bottom-up/top-down and right wall/left wall. Bottom-up/top-down is the basic procedure to search a multi-story building. Begin on the bottom floor and work your way up, one floor at a time, doing a rapid search of all the rooms. This is called a primary search. It is often done by emergency responders who work quickly to locate obvious victims. As safety allows, once you reach and search the top floor, descend one floor at a time, performing a secondary search. A secondary search is a more thorough and time-consuming evaluation of each room.

Right wall/left wall is the specific route you will take within each search area. Simply put, it means pick a wall and follow it around the entire room until it returns you to the doorway in which you entered. Using this technique will allow you to perform a complete search of an area in an efficient and methodical way. Because you pick a wall does not mean that you have to stay in physical contact with the wall or cannot deviate if you locate a victim or a hazard. It gives you a framework from which to work. Right wall/left wall also provides you an escape route. If you become disoriented you can reverse your direction and follow the path along the wall until you get back to the doorway and exit. As you search, you will:

- Encounter debris as you make your way through the damage. Use caution if you choose to move it. There could be hidden dangers or victims in close proximity of the debris.

- Feel doors with the back of your hand before opening. If the door is hot, there could be fire on the other side.

- Check under beds and in bathtubs, closets, and cabinets for small animals or children.

- While wearing full protective gear, move easily portable debris from your path as you go. This will help facilitate a rescue as well as give you a clear path of egress if you need to quickly evacuate.

- If you are working as a team and someone is outside in charge or in "command," advise them of your location and any victims or dangers you encounter. Use the A, B, C, D method's format to tell them where you are located.

- Mitigate any light hazards as you go without spending too much time on them as your priority is searching for victims.

- Look over, under, and around objects in each room.

Upon entering a search area, call out to victims. The easiest way to locate a victim is for them to tell you where they are. Shout, "Is there anyone in here?" or, "If you can hear me, come toward the sound of my voice." If anyone responds, make contact with them and quickly ascertain the extent of their injuries and try to find out if there is anyone else located inside. Depending on the information they give and the condition of the building, you may direct them outside as you continue your search.

If the victim's location is obscured, you can also utilize triangulation, or the use of multiple rescuers to view an area from several perspectives. Have three or more rescuers stand around the area and, guided by their view and the victim's sounds, light up the area. The lights from multiple angles will help to eliminate shadows and isolate where the victim is located. Triangulation is not a primary search method. It is typically used when other searches have been unsuccessful.

> **TIP:** If you find a victim, should you continue your search? No. Life safety is the highest priority. If you locate a victim, ask if there are others in the structure. Notify any other rescuers that you have located a victim and advise them if there are others believed to be inside. Move your victim to safety. Search with your eyes and ears. Rescue with your hands.

RESCUE

Locating victims in and around a structure that has been damaged means locating areas of entrapment. Victims could be caught under debris, injured, unconscious, or a combination of all of these. Your task begins with creating as safe a work environment as possible. Rescuers must work in teams and be in full protective gear. As previously mentioned, they should be wearing weather-appropriate clothing, sturdy footwear, leather work gloves, a dust mask, protective eyewear, and a helmet. The victims cannot receive help unless you can safely get to them without injury. Many well-intentioned volunteers have been injured or killed performing rescue operations because they weren't protected or mentally and physically prepared for the demands of disaster rescue.

An immense burden is placed on the body in times of crisis. The physical requirements are often greater than most people have experienced before. Even those in good physical condition can be put to the test. Enduring a disaster is different from the training people do in a gym or a fitness class. People act and react out of visceral desperation and concern. Chemicals flood the body, placing it in a heightened state both physically and mentally in a manner unlike what the majority of people have experienced. It taxes the body as well as emotional well-being.

A safe work environment also means creating a stable work area to increase your chances for a successful rescue and decrease the opportunity for rescuer injury. If you are in a situation where someone became trapped and is in need of rescue, you can assume that it is not a safe area. You and your team may have to create a work zone within the disaster area by lifting heavy objects or removing debris in order to get to the person.

One method of removing debris from a rescue area is to form a human chain. When there is a large amount of small, manageable debris, volunteers will line up, passing the debris from person to person to extract it from the rescue site. As you gather as many volunteers as you can to form the line, make sure that everyone is using as much safety gear as possible, especially gloves. The line should not restrict the path of travel and should allow for the removal of a victim or victims.

Often the debris left behind after a collapse is large, heavy, and difficult to maneuver. Freeing someone who may be trapped under or behind it can be daunting and dangerous. The sheer weight of collapsed structural members or heavy furniture may be more than you or your team can move. If that is the case you can use a system of *leverage* and *cribbing*.

When an object is too heavy to move you can use a lever to gain mechanical advantage. One end of a lever or pole is placed under the debris that needs to be moved. Place a stationary object underneath it to act as a fulcrum. When someone forces the lever down over the fulcrum, greater force is then applied to the end under the heavy object. Using leverage will help you move things that you couldn't ordinarily move with your own strength. Never place anyone or any body parts under the object until you have used cribbing.

Used in conjunction with leverage, cribbing is when a framework of wood, metal, or other material is stacked alternately to create a stable base for support. Cribbing can be used for disaster debris. There are two primary reasons to crib. The first is for safety reasons. When leverage is used there is the chance the lever could break or fail, causing the heavy weight to come crashing down, which could injure the victim further, hurt the rescuer, or both. If you build your cribbing as you raise the object, you prevent it from crushing someone or something that may be underneath it if it drops. The second reason is to capture progress. You may have to lift in increments. As you raise the heavy object, you can crib underneath it, . set it down on the cribbing, and reset your lever to raise it higher, cribbing as you go.

Leveraging and cribbing is a slow process. As you lift the object, place cribbing underneath that is capable of supporting its weight. In the fire service, we use the rule: "lift an inch, crib an inch." Make sure that as you lift one side of an object, you are not creating a dangerous or unstable condition at the other side of it. Slowly and methodically lift and crib just to the point where you can remove the victim. There is no need to raise any higher than is absolutely necessary. Once the victim has been safely removed, reverse the process. Never leave an unsafe condition behind.

> **TIP:** Your efforts should be limited to lightly trapped victims that will need minimal extrication and pose as little danger to the rescuers as possible.

RESCUE CARRIES AND DRAGS

Occasionally, once you remove debris and obstacles, victims may be able to remove themselves with little or no assistance. If the victim is not able to self-rescue, you will have to evaluate the situation and determine the best and safest means to remove them. The way you choose to remove a victim will depend on several factors:

- How many victims are in need of rescue?
- How many rescuers are available?
- What is the size and condition of the victim(s)?
- What are the condition and capabilities of the rescuers?
- What is the stability and safety of the immediate environment?

One-Person Carries

You may be the one-and-only available rescuer or, perhaps, your team may have had to split up to assist multiple people. In either case, you are acting alone and will want to choose the best method to extricate the victim from the structure. One-person carries can be extremely taxing on the rescuer. Adrenaline will work both for and against you. You may experience a surge of energy and strength, which leaves you prone to injury. It is also common, after a rush of adrenaline, to "run out of gas" quickly. You can tire and experience a rapid decrease in strength. Often rescuers will compensate by relying on fatigued larger muscle groups, like back muscles, to perform the brunt of the work, which exposes the rescuer to injury. Unless you are in a "life over limb" situation, these carries should only be conducted with the confidence that you will not cause greater injury to the victim. As always, keep your own safety a priority.

One person walk assist. If the victim simply needs help walking out, begin by helping them to their feet. Have the victim place his or her arm around your neck and hold on to their wrist. Place your other hand around their waist and assist them out of the building, moving as cautiously as the situation allows so as not to cause greater injury.

Cradle-in-arms carry. If the victim is a child you may be able to perform a cradle-in-arms carry. Kneel beside the child and place one arm under the back and one under the thighs. Lift slightly and roll the child into the hollow formed by your arms and chest. Lift with your leg muscles and carefully stand.

Arm carry. This is similar to a cradle-in-arms carry, only with a much heavier, adult victim. Reach around the victim's back and under their knees. They may be able to assist by putting an arm around your neck. Lift carefully with your legs and not your back. Despite how easy this looks in the movies, it should only be performed if the rescuer is very strong and the victim is not too large.

Firefighter carry. This is another carry that should only be done by a very strong rescuer and a smaller victim. With the victim in the lying-down position, hook your elbows under their armpits and raise them to a standing position. Place your right leg between the victim's legs. Grab the victim's right hand with your left. Squat down and wrap your right arm around the victim's right knee. Rise up and raise the victim's right thigh over your right shoulder. With the victim across your shoulders, carry them to safety.

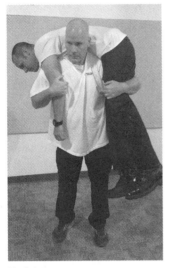
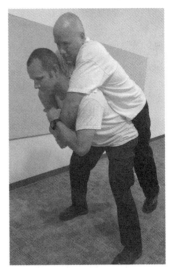

Firefighter carry | Pack strap carry

Pack strap carry. This carry could potentially be uncomfortable for the victim. Facing away from the victim, place their arms over your shoulders. Cross the victim's arms, grasping the opposite wrist, and pull them close to your chest. Squat slightly and drive your hips into the victim while bending at the waist. Balance the load on your hips as you lift up and carry.

Two-Person Carries

A victim is most safely and efficiently carried by two people. One-person carries should only be utilized when another rescuer is not available and the victim must immediately be moved to safety. By using two rescuers, obviously you share the weight of the load, making it less taxing. It also reduces rescuer fatigue, allowing a greater opportunity to remove multiple victims if needed. And finally, it is the safer alternative. One person attempting a carry is at the greatest risk of injury, and coordination becomes cumbersome when using more than two people.

Two-person walk assist. Each rescuer stands on either side of the victim and assists them to the standing position. Once fully upright, drape the victim's arms across the shoulders of the rescuers. Each rescuer puts their inside arm around the back of the victim and links them. Assist walking the victim to safety at their speed.

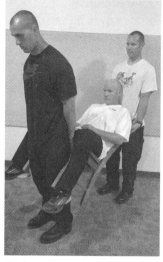
Chair carry

Two-handed seat carry

Chair carry. If you have a sturdy chair available, this method makes moving the victim much easier. Place the victim in a chair. The rescuer at the head grabs the chair, palms in, from the back and then leans the chair back on its hind legs. The second rescuer grabs the front legs of the chair. For short distances or on stairs, the second rescuer should face in. Over longer distances he or she should face out. At the command of the person on the head, stand and carry the victim out.

Two-person extremity carry. Help the victim to a seated position. The first rescuer kneels behind the victim and reaches under their arms, grasping their wrists. The second rescuer backs in between the victim's legs and grabs behind the knees. At the command of the rescuer at the head, stand using your legs and remove the victim.

Two-handed seat carry. The two- and four-handed carries should only be performed on fully conscious victims. To perform the two-handed seat carry, each rescuer kneels on either side of the victim. Raise the victim to the seated position and link arms behind their back. Place your free arms under the victim's knees and link arms. As you stand together, if the victim is conscious, have them place their arms around the rescuers for support.

Four-handed seat carry. Each rescuer will grab their own right wrist with their left hand. The two rescuers then grasp the left forearm of the other rescuer with their right hand. The rescuers squat down and allow the fully conscious victim to sit down on their interlocked hands. It is helpful if the victim can wrap their arms around the rescuers' shoulders to assist with stability and balance. The rescuers then carefully stand and walk to safety.

Litter Carry

Often there will be items or even debris around that you can use to your advantage. If you can locate two "poles" and a blanket, curtain, or any other piece of fabric large enough, you can quickly build an improvised stretcher to carry victims. There are multiple ways to construct a make-shift stretcher to carry victims that are not ambulatory. Utilizing an improvised stretcher will require a minimum of two rescuers or as many as six. Your first task is to locate the "poles." They can be sturdy pieces of lumber, tent poles, curtain rods, roof rack supports, or any other items that are sturdy enough to support the weight of a victim. Next you must find the fabric that makes up the middle part of the stretcher. You will want to find a blanket, tarp, sleeping bag, or any other fabric that can be used to support body weight.

1. Lay the blanket or other material flat on the ground.

2. Lay your "poles," dividing the blanket into thirds.

3. Ensure there is enough pole sticking out of either end for the rescuers to comfortably hold.

4. Fold one side of the cloth over a pole so that it reaches the other side.

5. Fold the other side back over the poles.

6. Continue to fold the fabric around the spaced poles as needed.

7. Place victim on the stretcher.

8. Carefully lift together in one motion.

A second method is to:

1. Fold the large piece of fabric in half.
2. Place the first pole in the middle of the fabric.
3. Fold the fabric in half again so that the pole is in the fold.
4. Place the second pole in the middle of the fabric parallel to the first.
5. Fold the fabric over the second pole back toward the first.
6. Place the victim on the stretcher.
7. Carefully lift together in one motion.

Litter carry

DRAGS

In some scenarios, assisting or carrying someone to safety cannot be done. While the safer option is to conduct a coordinated carry from a dangerous area to a secure location, time, terrain, or the lack of people available to assist can hinder any ideas for a methodical removal. For those times when you must quickly "grab 'n' go," dragging a victim is a last resort. The environment is usually treacherous, making everything dangerous for both the victim and the rescuer. However, when the situation dictates that you drag a victim to safety, there are a few ways to do it:

Shoulder drag. Place the victim in the seated position and align yourself behind them. Squat down and reach under the victim's arms. Grab the right wrist of the victim with your left hand and their left wrist with your right. From a squatting position, pull the victim's back into your chest. Rise up with your legs rather than your back and drag the victim to safety.

Blanket drag. Locate a blanket, curtain, tarp, or any other large piece of fabric. Tuck the blanket under the victim and roll the victim on to the center. Grasp the blanket behind the victim's head and drag them clear of the hazard.

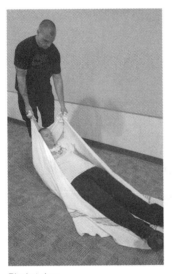

Blanket drag

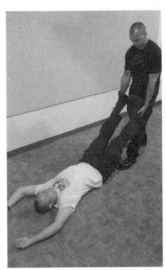

Feet drag

Feet drag. Dragging a victim by their feet is basically the last resort of the last resorts. You have no other way to move the victim to safety, but need to get them to a safer place. Place the victim on their back. Squat, grab the victim by the ankles, stand, and pull. Ideally you will pull them across a smooth, flat surface, but rarely in a disaster situation will you find a smooth, flat surface. Understand that by dragging a victim in this manner, the victim's head is prone to injury and their arms will drag away from the body, likely catching on doorways and debris. Do your best to limit additional injuries to the victim as you remove them from harm.

SUMMARY

In the aftermath of a disaster, search-and-rescue operations just happen. Family and friends immediately take inventory of their own circle and then begin searching for other survivors straight away. The best thing you can do for yourself, your family, and your neighbors is to prepare and educate yourself in advance of a crisis. Doing the greatest number of good for the greatest number of people can lead to making difficult choices. Obtain as much information as quickly as you can in order to adequately evaluate the risks involved. Know the limitations of yourself and those helping you. Perform a good size-up. Stabilize the incident. Then do a thorough search of the building, keeping rescuer safety a top priority. If you're not familiar with using leverage and cribbing techniques, practice using various items. As with other rescue procedures, the time to learn is not during the emergency event. Know how to use leverage and cribbing before the need arises. Then, choose the best method to remove victims from harm. By doing this you will be able to remove victims as quickly and safely as possible and minimize danger and injury to yourself and other rescuers.

CHAPTER 5
DISASTER MEDICAL OPERATIONS

I am a firefighter and an emergency medical technician. I am certified and medically trained to provide basic life support, which means, medically speaking, I stop a bad thing from getting worse and take people to the hospital. Without the benefit of being able to offer formal and specialized training, I cannot tell you how to heal, repair, or perform any other kind of invasive medical procedures. Despite what Hollywood would have you believe, that is done by people trained in advanced life support techniques in the hygienic confines of a hospital. What I *can* tell you is that disasters are messy and completely impartial to age, gender, race, or overall life potential. They strike without warning and there is no way to control them.

The winter of 2002 was an especially mild one for the Midwest. In fact, by the third week of January, temperatures had climbed into the 60s, which is a very rare and welcome occurrence. Then, on January 29, things began to drastically change. An arctic front drifted slowly and ominously across the plains. Mild rains blanketed the area as temperatures plunged. Ice began to form on everything, up to three inches in some places. Trees and power lines toppled to the ground under the weight of the ice. Buildings collapsed due to the hundreds of pounds of ice that accumulated on their roofs. The Midwest saw unseasonably mild temperatures drop to dangerous levels, causing sporadic fires and hundreds of thousands to be without power, including hospitals and nursing homes. I spent an entire 24-hour shift on an ambulance responding to a variety of weather-related emergencies, prioritizing them based on severity. In the middle of the night, as things began to settle down, our response shifted from emergency responses to checking the welfare of those with special medical needs. We conducted search and rescue in homes and buildings without power, often finding the elderly and sick who needed medical aid. With less than 48 hours' warning, the environment had diminished from pleasant to deadly.

Though advanced medical care is needed for many, pivotal actions taken in the immediate aftermath can reap long-term medical benefits. *Things* get broken or completely destroyed, but the heart and soul of disaster response is caring for the people that were affected. This forces us to make some crucial decisions.

In the early 1800s, Dominique Jean Larrey, a French surgeon in Napoleon's army, pioneered several methods still used in modern battlefield medicine. One of the most paramount procedures was his categorization of war casualties. He began treating the wounded by the severity of their injuries rather than by rank or how quickly the soldier could be returned to battle. Thus began the practice of triage.

Triage comes from the French word *trier*, which means "to sort." Triage is the process of dividing and prioritizing patients based on the urgency of their medical condition. On the surface, prioritizing victims seems like a simple concept: The more critical the patient, the higher priority their treatment. The reality is that, as previously mentioned, disasters are messy. Injuries are numerous and range from superficial to deadly and include everything in between. The sometimes overwhelming reality is people become victims concurrently. Suddenly there are many people requiring medical attention all at once. The number of victims will exceed the capacity to treat them. Prioritization is the first step. You must figure out how many people are injured and how you will utilize the limited available resources to render aid.

This chapter focuses on the initial phases of setting up medical treatment, from conducting triage to setting up treatment areas and working with emergency responders. If there are only a few victims, assuming you know basic first aid (see Chapter 6), your assessment can be focused and thorough. With several modern examples of large-scale disasters, such as the 2010 earthquake in Haiti and the Boston Marathon bombing in 2013, where the number of casualties were extensive, having a system in place to treat many patients simultaneously is crucial.

MEDICAL SIZE-UP

Sizing up an injured person is similar to other forms of size-up. Using verbal clues, visual clues, and previous training, you will be able to make an educated determination as to what their treatment priorities might be. Again, you are not expected to be a doctor. Even doctors have a full staff and the benefit of medical technology to understand what is happening in a patient's body. You will be in what is for all intents and purposes a war zone, rapidly making the best decision you can based on what you know and what you see.

A medical size-up begins with the scene of the incident. As previously discussed, your personal safety and the safety of other rescuers is your top priority. Before making any type of entry, make sure the scene is as safe as possible and utilize body substance isolation (BSI). BSI means wearing your personal protective equipment: medical gloves, eye protection, a filter mask, and anything else that you have available. Disaster scenes are often bloody and the risk of contamination is high. Blood-borne pathogens are clandestine and potentially lethal, so measures taken to protect yourself should not be considered optional.

Performing a medical size-up requires discipline. The chaos can be misleading. You know the expression, "the squeaky wheel gets the grease"? Often in a mass casualty situation, people will be crying and sometimes screaming. That could be from the mental and emotional trauma they just experienced, because a loved one is severely injured, or because of their own personal injury. If someone has the capacity to scream or cry out, their injuries may not necessarily be life threatening. A broken arm, while excruciatingly painful, is not considered life threatening, and while it may garner the loudest reaction, should not receive your immediate attention.

Do the greatest good for the greatest number of people. That begins with sorting and prioritizing the affected and injured. Find a starting point. It can be the front door or simply right where you stand, and commence the process of triage.

TRIAGE

Tend to patients as you encounter them, beginning with the assessment of the first patient you see. When there are many victims you simply cannot spend a lot of time on any one person. You will need the help of other volunteers.

As you approach the scene, there will likely be people self-evacuating. That is okay, and virtually impossible to contain even if you wanted to. Try to communicate with evacuating people to learn what happened, if there is anyone left at the scene, and what would be the quickest and safest way to get to the victims. That information may or may not be available, but any clues you can garner will be beneficial. In a best-case scenario you can corral the evacuees or walking wounded into one specific and safe area where they can be accounted for and evaluated.

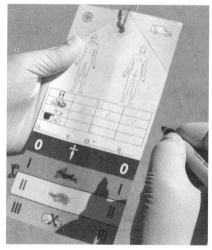

Triage tags are often used in mass casualty situations to quickly identify the severity of injuries as you simultaneously document patient information.

This is easier said than done due to people's tendency to leave a dangerous situation and keep on going until they are home or with family. Do the best you can. One thing to consider is that, depending on what event transpired, they could be contaminated. If possible, isolate those that have potentially been contaminated to avoid further exposure.

The victims you encounter will have a wide range of injuries. The first thing to do is to clear out anyone who can self-evacuate. Call out, "If you can hear me, come to the sound of my voice," or something similar. As the "walking wounded" begin to clear out, quickly interrogate them as to what happened, the extent of their injuries, and any other pertinent information. It is worth repeating that your best source of information is going to be the people that are/were there. They are going to possess the intimate knowledge that can be invaluable after a catastrophic event.

First responders often use "triage tags" in a mass casualty incident. The design of triage tags varies, but they are all sturdy tags that are used to document patient information. All of them use colors that correspond with their triage. Part of the tag is left with the patient so others can easily see that the victim has been evaluated and triaged. The other part of the tag remains with the rescuer to help maintain victim accountability. Triage tags can be ordered on the Internet and would be a beneficial addition to anyone's disaster preparation kit.

S.T.A.R.T. METHOD

Several methods are used to prioritize victims. Many professional emergency responders manage multiple casualty incidents using START triage: *simple treatment and rapid transport*. The START method utilizes color codes to quickly sort victims based on how they present to the rescuer. The color codes are:

Green: Minor Injuries

The walking wounded that self-evacuate are typically "green" patients. They will require little from you and can often treat themselves. Often, they will flee the scene altogether. With those that haven't fled, you can "voice triage." Call out to them and find to find out their status and the status of others. Verbally direct them. You may attempt to keep them around to assist you if their injuries allow. If not, do not encourage them to wander aimlessly around the scene. Relocate them to an area of refuge, protected from the weather, where they can receive treatment and recover.

Examples of "green" injuries are minor lacerations, sprains, bruises, and superficial burns.

Yellow: Delayed Treatment

If patients are triaged "yellow" or "delayed," it does not mean they are not injured. It means that, based on what you have observed, they are not at a high risk for early death and you can continue to assess other patients.

Examples of "yellow" injuries are fractures, moderate burns (that do not include the face, neck, or groin), and lacerations that have not cut into an artery.

Red: Immediate Treatment

The primary goal of sorting and prioritizing patients is to locate and help the "red" patients. Those are the people with potentially life-threatening injuries. One of the most difficult parts of the triage process is identifying the injured and moving on to the next. If you encounter a red victim and their injuries include an airway issue, you may reposition the airway (see Chapter 6). Otherwise, MOVE ON. Remember, you are doing the greatest good for the greatest number of people.

Examples of "red" injures are significant burns (especially to the face or neck), sucking chest wounds (a collection of air in the chest which causes part or all of a lung to collapse), shock, and severe external hemorrhages.

The sad reality is that there is no cardiopulmonary resuscitation (CPR) in a disaster. Even professional emergency responders will bypass CPR when the needs of victims outnumbers those that are able to offer aid. If someone is not breathing and/or their heart is not beating, they are considered deceased or type "black." Unfortunately, the time and resources to focus the type of attention required for someone who is in need of CPR are lacking. In a mass casualty environment, CPR is rarely effective and keeps rescuers from tending to potentially savable patients.

Black: Deceased

When you encounter a victim that is not breathing, you can try to reposition the airway by placing the person on their back and tilting their head up. If there are no respirations, attempt to reposition the airway one more time. If there is no spontaneous return of respirations, you must consider the person deceased. Leave them where they lie and mark them as deceased, either with a triage tag or a piece of paper or duct tape where you can write "deceased" or "black." (You may also take a moment to write the time and your initials so any rescuers who come along after you will know the patient had already been evaluated.)

Some people prefer to use the terminology rather than the color codes. If you are more comfortable using "minor," "delayed," and "immediate" rather than "green," "yellow," and "red," that is perfectly acceptable as long as everyone who is working with you understands and is using the same terminology.

The point of the START method is to keep the procedure for evaluating patients quick, thorough, and very simple. It has the added benefit of being a terminology used by professional emergency responders. Using the START method, the main concern is checking each person for breathing, a heartbeat, and good mental status. If even one of those presents to you as anything other than "normal," there is likely an issue that will require medical attention. Therefore, the easiest and quickest way to assess a patient in a disaster is to use RPM (respirations, perfusion, mental status).

Respirations. The average adult should have a resting respiratory rate of about 12 to 20 breaths per minute. Obviously, following a catastrophe, a slightly elevated respiratory rate should be expected. Counting respirations can be time-consuming. Use your experience and visual clues to make a determination. Keep it easy for yourself. The number of respirations isn't as important as the rate and quality of their breathing. Are they breathing normally? Slowly? Quickly? Is their breathing labored? Make a quick respiratory assessment based on what you see. Rapid breathing (over 30 breaths per minute) warrants a triage of red or immediate.

TRIAGE S.T.A.R.T. EVALUATIONS

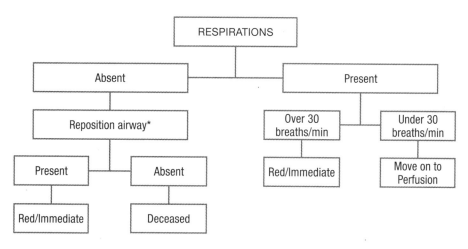

* Repositioning the airway will be covered in Chapter 6.

Perfusion. Perfusion is the body's process of delivering oxygenated blood to tissue and muscle. One fast way to check perfusion is to perform the blanch test for capillary refill. Push down on the victim's fingernail (or toenail) until color is lost. It will usually turn from pink to white as you apply pressure. Release the pressure and count how many seconds it takes until the original color returns. If it takes longer than two seconds, there is a compromise of circulation and the situation should be considered red/immediate.

You can also check for circulation by assessing a victim's pulse if you are comfortable with where and how to do so. In a disaster situation, though, a blanch test saves time. If you cannot check capillary refill due to nail polish, a pulse check would be appropriate.

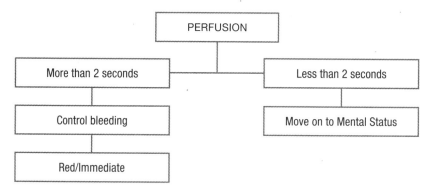

Mental status. To check someone's mental status you simply need to find out if they can answer simple questions. Avoid asking questions that you do not know the answer to, such as "What is your name?" or "What is your birthday?" to determine mental status. The name they give you may not be their name. You can ask "What day of the week is it?"; "Who is the president of the United States?"; or "Where are you right now?" An altered mental status could be caused by a variety of reasons, few of which will you be able to determine outside of a hospital setting.

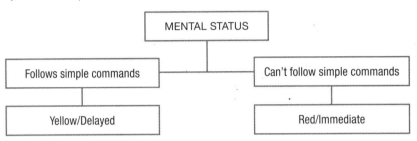

The general rule for RPM is *30-2-Can Do*. If their respirations are below 30, capillary refill is under 2 seconds, and they can answer simple questions, their treatment can be delayed for the sake of treating the known serious injuries in others. If they do not meet ALL THREE of the criteria in 30-2-Can Do, their injuries require immediate attention and receive a red or immediate triage.

Pitfalls

Common pitfalls tend to occur during the triage phase of a disaster. First and foremost is the lack of a decisive leader. Someone (preferably someone with past experience and training) should take charge. Without leadership there is no common plan of action. Instead there are freelance volunteers, each trying in their own way to help, with separate ideas of what needs to be done. They may ALL be correct ideas, but unless everyone has a common plan, nothing is efficient and tasks are duplicated or missed altogether.

The other main issue during triage is the propensity to provide treatment. It is easy to become focused on the child with a laceration to her forehead or the man screaming for help because his leg is fractured and temporarily lose sight of your objective, which is to sort and prioritize victims. Treatment will occur, but should not happen during triage.

ESTABLISHING TREATMENT AREAS

During the triage phase of a mass casualty incident, it is important that you not become involved with the treatment of patients. Your objective is to get to as many victims as possible, perform a quick assessment, and then assign them to an area based on their treatment needs. However, two treatment choices are acceptable during triage. You can 1) quickly apply a bandage or dressing to someone who is significantly bleeding and 2) adjust a person's airway (page 107) to see if spontaneous respirations will begin. In a perfect scenario, you would have an abundance of people and all the resources you need to triage and perform treatment. In reality, there will be a series of "this-will-have-to-do" solutions. Among the debris and sporadic influx of people who will be capable and willing to assist, you will need to designate areas of treatment for the wounded. I have seen neighboring houses, businesses, tarps laid out in the yard, and even vehicles used. You should weigh the needs of the possible treatment demands with what you have available and make an educated decision.

When selecting a treatment area, ask yourself these questions:

- How many patients can I expect?
- Is there a safe location nearby that can accommodate that number?
- Will my area be uphill and upwind from the hazard?
- Can my treatment area expand as the number of patients expand?
- If it is a building, is the building structurally sound?
- If it is not in a building, is the area free from other hazards?
- Will weather affect my location?
- Is the location I select easy for patients to find and access?
- Does the location allow for access and egress for transport?

SECONDARY DEVICES

In these times of rampant terrorism, it is an unfortunate reality that we must prepare for man-made catastrophes. The bad guys are becoming more and more creative with their destructive and deadly actions. The attacks on 9/11, the bombings of the Athens, Greece, police station during the 2004 Olympics, and the bombs detonated at the Boston Marathon in 2013 are prime examples that their intent is not only to send a message, but to injure and take lives. A common thread among these examples is the use of secondary devices. A terrorist will create an explosion, be it from a backpack bomb or an airplane flown into a building. Then, after a prescribed amount of time, when volunteers and emergency rescuers flood the scene to assist, a second device will detonate with the intent to kill more citizens along with rescuers and create unbridled fear. It is profoundly effective in their determination to create destruction and chaos.

When choosing treatment areas, particularly after a terrorist event or civil unrest, be aware of the possibility that secondary devices will be present. Rarely are they set to go off at the exact location of the initial incident but rather very near it, where rescuers are likely to be congregating and working. Obviously, there is no way to know for certain that an area is safe from a secondary device, but in the case of a man-made catastrophe, be aware of the possibility and take whatever steps are necessary to keep yourself and your treatment area away from further harm.

IMMEDIATE AND DELAYED TREATMENT

As you set up treatment areas, keep the red patients separate from the yellow patients. This will prevent wandering victims from disrupting your accountability system. Although, as needed, you can utilize your green and, if possible, yellow victims to assist in caring for the red patients. It complicates your accountability a bit, but in a disaster situation, everyone is doing the best that they can with what is available.

Red patients who require immediate treatment should be placed close enough to the incident site that they can be easily moved to the treatment area, but also have access to an evacuation route where ambulances or other vehicles can transport them to medical facilities.

MORGUE

Catastrophic events result in a vast number of casualties. Deceased victims found during search-and-rescue operations should be moved or touched as little as possible. Officials will need to document the victims' location and cause of death. In addition, your resources will be limited, and removing and securing the deceased will require more assets than you will likely have available to you.

As you set up treatment areas, you will have to identify a location to be used as a temporary morgue. The morgue is used for those who pass away in the treatment areas. The morgue should be out of sight of the treatment areas and out of view of the general public. It should be in as secure an area as possible to protect the dignity of the deceased. Because of the sad prevalence of looting, even of dead bodies, assign someone to watch over the morgue. That person may not be able to stop a determined looter, but their mere presence may be enough to keep honest people honest.

SANITATION

An easily dismissed topic in disaster preparation is sanitation and waste disposal. We often ponder what to do to survive without giving much consideration to the safe and proper disposal of trash, blood, urine, feces, etc. All warrant disposal consideration.

Numerous wounded people, along with countless rescuers, create a hazardous environment. Maintaining high levels of personal protection and cleanliness is important before, during, and after the incident, both for rescuers and victims. The lack of sanitation is the leading cause of disease following a disaster and can result in more deaths than the event itself.

As victims and rescuers assemble and begin the process of cleaning and treating wounds, contaminated clothing, sheets, and medical supplies accumulate. Without proper sanitation procedures, these items can be extremely harmful, as they contain an abundance of body fluids such as blood or body waste. Containing and properly disposing of the waste or fluids, or any items that come into contact with them, is critically important.

Hygiene and sanitation begin with basic hand washing. Clean water from faucets can be rare following a disaster due to the fact that many of the water lines become damaged or the water supplies tainted. Use bottled or sanitized water for both drinking and cleaning. Keeping your hands clean and protected will prevent you from contracting or spreading any unwanted bacteria. In some disaster response areas, I have seen temporary hand-washing stations that consist of a large jug or bucket of clean water, soap, and disposable drying towels. If soap and water are not available, use alcohol-based hand sanitizer. When coming in contact with victims, ensure you have appropriate gloves (leather work gloves or, if rendering treatment, medical gloves) and make every attempt to maintain clean and protected hands.

According to the CDC, you should wash your hands:

- Before, during, and after preparing food
- Before eating food
- After using the toilet
- After changing diapers or cleaning up any human waste
- Before and after caring for someone who is sick
- After blowing your nose, coughing, or sneezing
- After touching an animal or animal waste
- After touching garbage
- Before and after rendering first aid

When it comes to trash, the thought process is reduce, reuse, recycle. Reduce the amount of trash you create, reuse what you can, particularly with limited supplies, and recycle the things that can be reused.

Human waste can carry nasty bugs like salmonella, intestinal parasites, and a slew of other pathogens that can cause sickness and even death. Knowing what to do with it is more important than most people realize. Urine isn't really an issue as long as no one is leaving it near a water source. Feces, on the other hand, must be managed. Several methods are available to contain feces.

The first is to use the bucket-and-bag technique. Place a trash bag in a bucket (with a lid) and use that for defecation. Once finished, place the lid back on the bucket. After each use, or whenever you need to dispose of it, you remove the bag, tie it off, and bury it safely away from the recovery area. Another option is the use of camping or compost toilets that contain and sometimes sanitize feces. The final method is to simply dig a hole in the ground. Dig it deeper than you think you will need to and cover it after it is no longer needed. The management of human waste, of both victims and rescuers, must be managed as carefully as any other part of your response.

Finally, there will be blood. Bloody victims, bloody clothing, bloody rescuers, and bloody equipment. It is not news that blood-borne pathogens are extremely dangerous. The safe disposal of biohazard materials tainted with body fluids is paramount. These vital steps should be taken to clean up blood and other potentially infectious fluids:

Disinfect. Any area that has or may have come into contact with blood or another potentially infectious fluid should be thoroughly disinfected. Make a 1:10 bleach solution (1 cup bleach to 10 cups water), let it sit for 30 minutes after mixing, and use it to clean and sanitize any offending area All cleaning supplies should be collected in a plastic bag, sealed shut, and thrown away. Clean anything that will be reused, such as beds or equipment, with the same 1:10 bleach solution and allow to sit for 20 minutes.

Properly dispose of supplies. Anything sharp (needles, razors, etc.) should be placed in a sturdy plastic container, preferably with a lid, that can resist puncture. Any soft supplies such as fabric, shoes, gauze, etc., can be collected in a plastic bag.

Mark off a biohazard zone. Any waste containers or bags should be collected in an area that is marked as a biohazard zone and completely restricted from contact with anyone. For example, at earthquake-recovery sites, dumpsters have been used and clearly marked as biohazard waste containers. If you choose to do that, make sure the dumpster is clearly marked. It should not located on a paved surface. If it is, place the dumpster downwind and downhill from action areas to avoid contamination in case of leakage. Another option is to bury or burn the waste in a safe manner, distant from any potential contact or cross contamination.

SUPPLIES

The rescue-and-recovery effort will be demanding on many levels. In addition to manpower, a vast amount of supplies will be required. Rescuers will need personal protective gear and equipment, victims will need first aid supplies, and everyone involved may need food, water, shelter, lighting, safety and sanitation equipment, and personal hygiene items. As volunteers arrive to assist with the efforts, they may bring items from home or procured on the way to the site. If not, as the situation allows, you will want to send a person/people to acquire supplies. Assemble the supplies in a central and easily accessible area that is known by all who may need them.

Basic First Aid Checklist

- ❑ 2x2-inch gauze
- ❑ 4x4-inch gauze
- ❑ Alcohol-based hand sanitizer
- ❑ Aloe vera gel
- ❑ Antacid
- ❑ Antibacterial ointment
- ❑ Antidiarrheal medication
- ❑ Aspirin
- ❑ Benadryl
- ❑ Burn dressing
- ❑ Butterfly bandages
- ❑ Cold and flu medication
- ❑ Cotton swabs
- ❑ Emergency dental kit
- ❑ Eye drops
- ❑ First aid field guide
- ❑ Heat packs
- ❑ Ice packs
- ❑ Insect bite treatment
- ❑ Medical tape
- ❑ Normal saline
- ❑ Pain reliever (Ibuprofen, acetaminophen, etc.)
- ❑ Petroleum jelly
- ❑ PPE (gloves, mask, safety glasses, etc.)
- ❑ Prescription medication
- ❑ Roll gauze
- ❑ Snake bite kit
- ❑ Superglue
- ❑ Thermometer (with protective covers)
- ❑ Trauma shears
- ❑ Triangular bandages (with safety pins)
- ❑ Tweezers
- ❑ Variety pack of adhesive bandages in assorted sizes

Personal Protective Equipment (PPE) Checklist

- ❑ Hard hat
- ❑ Hearing protection
- ❑ Leather work gloves
- ❑ Medical gloves
- ❑ Respirator
- ❑ Safety glasses

- ❏ Sturdy footwear
- ❏ Sunscreen
- ❏ Weather-appropriate clothing

Equipment Checklist

- ❏ Axe
- ❏ Basic tools
- ❏ Broom
- ❏ Buckets
- ❏ Communication radio
- ❏ Duct tape
- ❏ Flashlights with batteries
- ❏ Generator and fuel
- ❏ Ink pens and writing paper
- ❏ Knife
- ❏ Litter (two poles and a sturdy blanket)
- ❏ Matches or lighters
- ❏ Permanent markers
- ❏ Plastic bags
- ❏ Pry bar
- ❏ Rope
- ❏ Tarps

Sanitation Checklist

- ❏ Bleach
- ❏ Buckets
- ❏ Large plastic trash bags
- ❏ Scrub brushes
- ❏ Soap
- ❏ Towels and rags

DOCUMENTATION

The three incident priorities, life safety, incident stabilization, and property conservation, are written in stone. There is also a fourth, often unmentioned, priority—documentation. Documentation will in no way take precedence or replace any of the three incident priorities, but is extremely important nonetheless. A crisis creates a chaotic scene and just as volunteers and victims must be organized, so must information.

Disasters are interesting in the fact that as they occur, everyone runs away from them. After it has passed, everyone runs toward the site of the disaster. People frantically search for friends and loved ones or any information as to their whereabouts. Do not think for a moment that you can try to keep a mother whose child may be in a collapsed building away from a scene, let alone dozens of family members or concerned citizens. The best assistance you can provide will be your ability to inform them. With accurate information you can tell concerned family members that their loved one is in the triage area or has been transported to a specific hospital. With accurate and up-to-date documentation, you can avoid unnecessary anxiety and injuries by keeping concerned family away from the danger area.

Whether you have a fully charged functioning tablet or a rock that you can scratch notes onto concrete with, you will want to document pieces of information. Relying on memory alone lends itself to failure. There is too much going on too quickly to accurately remember all of the information you will want to recollect. Documentation does not have to be anything formal. It can be a collection of your own notes and the compilation of documents from other rescuers that you accumulate and organize after you have a handle on things.

The term "documentation" lends itself to writing things down. Sometimes the easiest way to document, rather than with pen and paper, is to utilize the available technology. Take pictures and video. Often, visual documentation accompanies, accentuates, and can even provide more accurate information than scribbled notes or formally written documentation. Pictures or video of the scene can provide investigators with clues and evidence of what occurred prior to their arrival. You can also take pictures of the injured to later help identify who exactly had come through your triage and treatment areas. Some rescuers video record their searches to allow those in charge, outside of the structure, to see the extent of interior damage and the victims still within.

Regardless of what method you use to document, you will want to record names, events, locations, and procedures as soon as practically possible, either during or immediately after the incident. In a perfect scenario, there will be someone available to document information from the event itself through post-incident efforts. Typically, though, the few available volunteers will be busy with other more critical tasks.

Here are some general recommended guidelines when documenting disaster response activities:

- Do not speculate.
- Record only the facts.

- Do not elaborate.

- Do not relate unqualified opinions.

Within those guidelines, your documentation should be as detailed or as general as the situation allows. During most disaster recoveries, documentation is sporadic and incomplete, if it happens at all, and this scarcity of information becomes a hindrance when emergency responders arrive and begin to take over the scene. Proper tracking of the event and victims both streamlines the recovery process and helps investigators re-create the scene to determine the whats, whens, hows, and whos.

At a minimum, your documentation should focus on people; first, the victims, and second, the volunteer responders. Whatever the situation that caused the destruction, there will undoubtedly be mass casualties. Recording and tracking them can be a struggle amid the chaos of everything. The bottom line is to do the best that you can to note information directly related to victims and rescue teams.

The following questions ascertain important information that emergency responders will want to know as they take over the scene:

General

- What happened?

- Where did it take place/what was affected?

- When did it occur?

- Was there any warning?

- Did appropriate alarms function properly?

- Is everyone accounted for?

- Was an emergency response/evacuation plan implemented?

- Has the situation been mitigated or is there still a hazard or threat?

Victims

- How many people are injured?

- Where are they located?

- Are there still victims inside the structure/site?

- Where and how were they injured?

- How severe are the injuries?
- Has anyone been transported to a hospital or relocated?
- If so, who and where?
- What are their names and contact information?
- How many people are deceased?
- Where are they located?
- What caused their death?
- Have they been left in place or relocated?

Rescuers

- How many volunteers are assisting with the effort?
- Are they working in teams or individually?
- What were their assignments?
- What were their findings?
- Where are they located now?
- What are their names and contact information?

Supplies

- What supplies have you been using?
- From where did you obtain them?
- Is there a central supply location? Where?
- What supplies are needed for victims?
- What supplies are needed for rescuers?

This seems like a lot of information and it can be difficult to obtain all of it. You may not be able to practically find out all of this information. You may not even know the answer to many of the important questions, but any information you can have documented, be it in written, photographic, or video format, will greatly help family members trying to locate loved ones, emergency responders as they arrive, and investigators as they re-create the scene to learn what happened and what steps can be taken so that it doesn't happen again.

WORKING WITH EMERGENCY RESPONDERS

In the direst of circumstances, when people are at their most desperate hour, when circumstances are beyond their capacity and they have no one else to call, they dial 911. As quickly as possible, emergency responders arrive to control the chaos. That's what we do: control chaos. I am a second-generation firefighter and, with almost twenty years in the fire service myself, I have seen my share of chaos. There are times, though, when an event overwhelms the system and there is more chaos than there are professional emergency responders. That is when volunteer responders rise to the occasion and intervene.

As an emergency responder myself, I can tell you that when an event is so big or so widespread that crews cannot get to everyone who needs help right away, it is disheartening. Our only hope is that there are people there to help until we can arrive.

Recently, during a particularly rainy spring, flood waters overflowed their banks and enveloped subdivisions. Our emergency response crews were doing their best to go from house to house to ensure everyone was safe. Because this is a labor- and time-intensive operation, the waters had receded before all the homes could be checked. During the search, I made contact with a small group of people from within the subdivision who wanted to help. I divided them up into teams and gave them a crash course in what dangers to look for, what to do if they located a victim, and how to communicate with me. Because of their assistance, the homes were checked in a fraction of the time, utilities were shut off, which eliminated many hazards, and we were happy to report that there were no casualties, only a few minor injuries.

When an emergency crew arrives on the scene they want to know four things: what happened, what was done prior to their arrival, are the measures that have been put in place being successful, and what changes to the plan are needed. Since the procedures outlined in this book are the ones taught by many fire departments around the nation, you can benefit from common tactics, common goals, and common terminology. When that first fire truck or ambulance arrives, you will be able to use words like *size-up*, *casualties*, and *triage*. Those are terms that emergency responders use daily. Speaking the same language helps to streamline the transition process.

Do not be offended if emergency responders arrive on the scene, thank you for your efforts, and relieve you from your position. There are liability issues in place as well as the unknown status of the training and physical and mental abilities of the general public. I've seen that transition done politely and I've seen it done swiftly and bluntly without niceties. It will depend on the arriving officer in charge and how the situation stands upon their arrival.

In other instances, they will be happy to have your assistance and will put you to work. In fact, if you've done things correctly, they may just continue the process that you have already begun. Either way, your effort is invaluable to affected victims

SUMMARY

In a disaster, you can be certain of two things: The number of victims will exceed the capacity for treatment and survivors will help other survivors. Most volunteer rescuers are untrained and ill-prepared to undergo the demands that will be placed on them. An insistence on the use of PPE and strong leadership will offer the best and safest scenario for them. Disaster medical operations begin with those willing to help and succeeds with a sound plan of action.

Effective medical treatment will begin with the establishment of structure. The victims will be numerous and the urge to help everyone all at once, while natural, must be done in the proper context. The best way to help as many people as possible is to do rapid, effective, and thorough triage. Begin with voice triage and call to the walking wounded. Once they are evacuated, follow a systematic route and use RPM to sort and prioritize. Establish treatment areas where "red or "immediate" patients receive first treatment and transport priority. Document as you go or as circumstances will allow. Do the greatest amount of good for the greatest number of people.

CHAPTER 6
DISASTER FIRST AID

The simple fact that you are reading this book means you recognize the potential for a catastrophic event and have more than a passive interest in rendering aid if one were to occur. A primary part of that aid will come in the form of treating the wounded. It should come as no surprise that modern disaster trauma care traces its origins back to military medicine. Throughout history, soldiers were treated on the battlefields in less-than-ideal circumstances. While there probably won't be an enemy hurling gunfire at you in the vast majority of disaster medical situations you may find yourself, the circumstances can be astonishingly similar. The number of patients will outnumber the capacity for treatment. There will be limited supplies and a staggering lack of formally trained people to assist. Aid will come in the form of survivors doing the best they can to help each other.

During World War II, the United States Army assigned soldiers who were not physicians to the trenches. They were given a crash course in battlefield medicine, issued a first aid kit, and sent to war. Following an extreme weather event or man-made disaster, the sights, smells, terrain, and destruction will parallel some of the same obstacles that soldiers experience following a battle. A devastating catastrophe that comes upon you by wind, rain, fire, or even other people will send you reeling in the aftermath. Once you're sure you are OK and able and willing to help others, you can begin to render treatment.

This chapter will discuss airway, breathing, and circulation; bleeding control; broken bones; burns; medical emergencies; physical trauma; shock; and sprains and strains.

PERSONAL PROTECTIVE EQUIPMENT

Before administering any type of first aid, follow the lead of professional healthcare providers and use full personal protective equipment. Even the most basic PPE provides important barriers to prevent injury and infection. Personal protection begins (and ends) with clean hands. You should wash your hands thoroughly before and after rendering any kind of first aid. If clean warm water and soap are not available, use waterless hand sanitizer. Then, don medical gloves. Many people have an allergy to latex, so the more hypoallergenic nitrile or vinyl gloves are commonly used.

Any time blood or other body fluids may become airborne, a medical mask should be worn to prevent infectious fluids from being splashed into the nose or mouth. Eye protection should also be worn for the same reasons. Eyes provide a direct path to the bloodstream and should be protected.

Utilize all available PPE. Medical scenes are unpredictable and can be extremely dangerous for the rescuer. All available precautions should be taken to avoid additional injuries and the transmission of blood-borne pathogens.

ABCS

Regardless of the illness or injury, or its cause, there are priorities in medical treatment. "ABC" breaks this down to the simplest of terms. "A" refers to airway. If someone is not breathing, nothing else matters. Sometimes an airway can be blocked or simply in a position not conducive for respirations. A patent airway must be established, and you must ensure they are *using* that airway. "B" is for breathing. Check for breathing. IF they have an open airway and IF they are breathing, move on to "C," for circulation. Is their heart beating? Once the ABCs are established, you can move on to treat other injuries, but unless they have an open airway, are breathing, and have a heartbeat, nothing else matters.

In multi-casualty events, cardiopulmonary resuscitation (CPR) is not performed by emergency responders. This is a blunt statement that seems shocking and calloused. Unfortunately, time and resources aren't available to commit to performing CPR. Victims must have a patent airway AND be breathing AND have a pulse in order to receive treatment. If any of those are missing, the victim is considered deceased and protocol calls for moving on to the next victim. In a few exceptions, minor maneuvers, such as repositioning the airway, can be done quickly to try to rectify the issue; otherwise, as difficult as it may be, you should refer back to achieving your goal of doing the greatest number of good for the greatest number of people.

Airway and breathing. The human airway consists of a few major components: the nasal airway, the oral airway, the trachea, and the lungs. Together they are responsible for introducing oxygen to the body and into the blood cells. The airway can be obstructed by a number of things. Food is the most common obstruction, but is rarely the cause in a disaster. If someone isn't moving air, it is typically because something happened to one of the components that make up the "airway." To inspect for a patent airway and breathing:

1. Check for responsiveness. Shake the person and ask, "Are you okay?"

2. If there is no reply, perform a head tilt/chin lift. Place one hand on the forehead and two fingers under the chin. Tilt the jaw upward and the head slightly back.

3. Look, listen, and feel. Look for a chest rise, listen for air exchange, and feel for abdominal movement.

4. If, after performing the head tilt/chin lift, the victim does not start breathing, return the airway to its normal position and repeat steps 2 and 3.

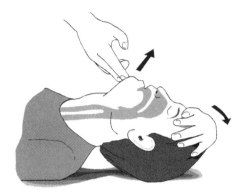

Head tilt/chin lift

If spontaneous respirations do not return after checking the airway, repositioning, and checking again, the victim should be considered deceased. When there is the possibility of a spinal injury, a head tilt/chin lift should not be done. Any patient with a suspected injury to the spine should be moved as little as possible. As an alternative, a "jaw thrust" maneuver should be performed, which opens the airway without moving the neck.

To perform a jaw thrust:

1. Grasp the angles of the lower jaw and lift with both hands.

2. If the victim's mouth is closed, open it with your thumbs.

If the patient is breathing, they will have a pulse. However, this does not work the other way around. It sounds confusing, but it is simple, really. A person cannot breathe without a pulse. If breaths are present or become present when you open the airway, you should still check circulation for rate and quality.

Circulation. Check circulation by ensuring there is a heartbeat. This is first done visually. If the victim is talking, moving, or breathing, they certainly have a heartbeat. If they are unresponsive, you must perform a pulse check. There are many places around the body to check for a pulse, but the two easiest and most common ways are to check for a radial or carotid pulse.

A radial pulse check is performed at the radial artery. Turn the victim's arm palm up while it rests on a flat surface with the elbow no more than slightly bent. Place your index and middle fingers on the wrist, just below the base of the thumb. Press slightly. If you do not feel a pulse, press slightly harder or move your fingers a short distance to try to locate the radial artery.

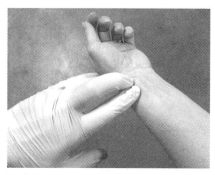

Radial pulse

To check a pulse at the carotid artery, place your index and middle fingers on the neck in the crease that is on either side of the esophagus. The carotid pulse is typically very strong and easy to find. You shouldn't have to press very hard to locate it.

The starting point for every victim assessment, establishing the ABCs often happens without conscious thought. If you see someone moving or crying out, you can assume they are breathing and have a heartbeat. After asking someone where they hurt, any response confirms their ABCs are intact and you can then focus your treatment on the specific injuries.

THE GOLDEN HOUR

The human body is surprisingly resilient. It can take a fair amount of physical insult and still manage to keep itself protected. During an average lifetime, the body is placed under a steady barrage of abuse, from run-of-the-mill illnesses to bumps, bruises, and falls. But built-in mechanisms and systems are genetically programmed to keep you alive.

Trauma, which takes on many forms, is something else altogether. The most common injuries that occur during a disaster are the result of physical trauma. Blunt force injuries, broken bones, burns, and penetrating injuries inundate treatment areas. Broken bones and injuries to the neck and back are far more common than medical issues such as allergic reactions or heart attacks. An understanding of the recognition and treatment of physical trauma is of the utmost importance in the minutes and hours following a disaster.

In emergency medicine there is a time period known as "the golden hour." The concept originated during World War I and has been an objective for emergency responders ever since. The golden hour refers to the 60 minutes immediately following a traumatic injury. A victim's chance of survival decreases greatly if they have not received professional medical care within that hour. With advances in medicine since World War I, the golden hour is more of general guideline and a goal than a hard-and-fast rule. Rapid treatment certainly doesn't guarantee anything, but offers the best chance of survival in a traumatic situation.

NECK AND BACK INJURIES

The spinal cord is basically an extension of the brain. People often think of the spinal cord as synonymous with the back. While that is true, the spinal cord is so much more. It runs from your head to your bottom and provides support and stability, but more importantly, acts as a message delivery system for the entire body. Vital bodily systems, including muscle coordination and even the impulse to breathe, are coordinated via the spinal cord. There are numerous and significant reasons for administering special care to someone with a suspected spinal injury. Any injury to the neck or back should be treated as if it is an injury to the spinal cord.

Without advanced medical equipment, there is no way to tell for certain the difference between a muscular injury and a fracture. Therefore, you should err on the side of caution and take all neck and back injuries seriously. Nothing can be done outside of a hospital to "repair" such an injury. With minor trauma to the neck or back comes localized pain. Anyone who has experience with back pain understands that it can affect many things that we take for granted: breathing, movement, even finding positions of comfort to sit or lie down. Major injuries may cause paralysis or death. Great caution should be given when handling someone with a neck or back injury.

Whether you are at the scene of a car accident and want to help by rendering aid before emergency responders arrive or are wading through the aftermath of a crippling weather event and are dealing with mass injuries, your primary goal for anyone who has sustained a spinal injury is to ensure they have their ABCs and to limit their movement.

The symptoms of a spinal injury can be misleading. Substantial damage to the spine can initially appear as localized pain. Other times, excruciating pain can simply be the result of a pulled muscle. Because you may not have the level of training or necessary equipment to adequately diagnose a spinal injury, any neck or back injury should be treated as a "worst-case scenario." Symptoms of a neck or back injury are:

- pain (back, neck, or circumferential chest pain)
- muscle spasms on either side of the spine
- numbness or tingling of the extremities
- paralysis

The treatment of any neck or back injury (once the ABCs have been evaluated) is primarily immobilization. Any movement by the injured person should be kept to an absolute minimum. Movement can cause a spinal injury to worsen and should only happen if they are being transported to medical care or if they are in danger where they are. The victim should not ambulate themselves, but should remain as motionless as possible and allow rescuers to move them.

Identify the potential severity of a spinal injury by assessing motor function or determining if a victim can move and feel their extremities. Ask them to wiggle fingers or toes of each hand and foot. Pinch a finger on each hand and a toe on each foot and ask if they can feel it. The loss of feeling or movement is indicative of a spinal injury, and even if they have maintained motor function, your treatment remains the same.

- Lay the patient on a hard, flat surface such as a long spine board, a door, a large piece of paneling, or anything that will allow the patient to be relocated by rescuers for treatment and/ or transport.

- Place soft packing on either side of the head to prevent side-to-side movement. Clothing, towels, or sheets work well for this purpose.
- Monitor the patient for any changes.
- Move the patient only when absolutely necessary.
- If the patient needs to vomit, roll the head, neck, and body as a single unit. At least two people are needed to perform this: one supporting the head as the other person rolls the shoulders and hips.

An injury to the spine can be one of the most difficult to diagnose and treat. Unless there are specific complaints or deficits (such as loss of movement or sensation in the arms or legs), you can only assume by what is known as "mechanism of injury" that a spinal injury may have occurred. Mechanism of injury refers to the circumstances in which an injury occurred. If someone fell from a distance greater than twice their height or suffered some other form of blunt force trauma, assume that an injury to the spine may have happened. They should be immobilized and transported to an emergency room as soon as possible. Until they are ready for transport, move a victim with a spinal injury as little as possible and only when absolutely necessary.

BROKEN BONES

Fractures can have varying degrees of severity. A broken bone in the hand or foot, while very painful, is typically minor. The fracture of a bone in the skull, upper leg, or pelvis can be extremely dangerous. Skull fractures can infringe on the brain, affecting function, and an upper leg or pelvic fracture can lead to significant internal bleeding.

Following a disaster, treatment areas see the entire gamut of broken bones, from less important slight cracks to critical long bone fractures. Falls, collapses, flying debris, physical altercations, and vehicle collisions are just a few causes of traumatic injury causing broken bones in a calamitous event.

A broken bone can have many "looks." It is possible to have no exterior visual clues. On the surface, the site can appear perfectly normal, although the patient will be experiencing localized pain in the area. Most often, though, there is redness and swelling at the site, indicating a fracture. At the other end of the spectrum, an "open" fracture has pierced the skin and the bone is exposed.

Any time there is an obvious or suspected broken bone, you must first determine the location and severity. Then, render appropriate treatment as follows and relocate the patient to a medical facility as soon as possible.

- Check the ABCs (page 107).

- Control bleeding by applying direct pressure to the wound and elevating, unless this causes pain to the patient.

- Examine for other, potentially more serious injuries.

- Immobilize the fracture with a splint (see splinting).

- Wrap ice or an ice pack in a cloth and apply to the site to reduce swelling.

- Take steps to prevent shock. Lay the person flat on their back and elevate their feet about 12 inches. This is done ONLY if there is no head, neck, or back injury or if it doesn't cause pain.

Do not do the following:

- Move the person unless the fracture has been stabilized.

- Move or reposition a person with a spinal injury.

- Move a person with an upper leg, hip, or pelvis injury unless absolutely necessary.

- Test a bone's ability to move.

- Attempt to straighten a bone or change its position unless circulation has been compromised.

- Touch an exposed bone. It should be lightly rinsed to remove debris and covered as it is with sterile dressing.

SPLINTING

When you "splint" a broken bone, you are stabilizing the injury and protecting it from further damage. The best way to do that is to place a firm object under the injury site, preferably one that conforms to the shape of the injured extremity. I have created makeshift splints out of pillows, newspapers, and even small branches.

Ideally you want to splint the joint above and below the fracture site. For example, if the person has a fractured forearm, you will splint the wrist to the elbow. This isn't always possible, particularly when supplies are limited, but should be done whenever possible. Then, use a bandage or cloth to wrap the extremity to the object. You 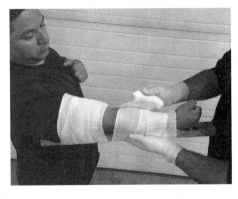 should wrap firmly, while being careful not to impede circulation. After you finish wrapping the splint, ask the patient to move their fingers or toes and check capillary refill (page 91) to ensure you haven't wrapped the splint too tightly and restricted blood flow. If their arm or leg begins to tingle or lose sensation, loosen the wrap.

If the elbow is not involved, place a fractured arm against the chest and wrap it around the body, effectively using the victim's torso as part of the splint. This will provide stability and protection.

STRAINS AND SPRAINS

A strain affects the ligaments, the tissue that connects bone to bone around a joint. A sprain affects the fibrous tissues, or tendons, that connect muscle to bone.

Strains and sprains usually affect the knees and ankles. They occur often during the heat of a disaster when people are placed in perilous and sometimes panic-induced situations. Rapid movements over uneven terrain create an environment conducive to tendons and/or ligaments being ripped from the bone. Strains and sprains are painful and hinder any kind of movement, which is particularly an issue during an evacuation scenario. Generally speaking, the greater the swelling, the greater damage that has been done. To treat strains and sprains, use the acronym RICE.

R: Rest the injured limb as much as possible.

I: Ice should be wrapped in a cloth and placed over the injury to reduce swelling.

C: Compress the area with a bandage from a first aid kit.

E: Elevate the injured limb as much as possible to allow gravity to assist you in keeping the swelling down.

BLEEDING CONTROL

Whether a hurricane just blew through your city, a civil uprising erupted in your neighborhood, or you are simply working in the yard, the potential for a bleeding injury is ever present. Following a crisis, bleeding control may be the most common first aid action you perform.

The average adult has about five liters of blood in their body. The body can compensate for a fair amount of blood loss, but there is a break-over point. Obviously, the more blood that is lost, the greater danger to the victim. As the amount of blood loss reaches one liter, death can occur. Blood has a tendency to thin out and spread, so bleeding can often look worse than it is. Since you cannot adequately measure blood loss, it should be taken seriously and treated quickly.

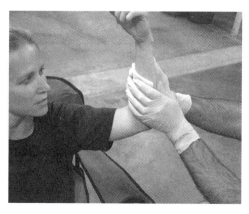

First and foremost, utilizing PPE is extremely important when dealing with blood. The pathogens that may be present in blood can be deadly. You must take all measures to protect yourself as well as your patients. Use medical gloves, often made of nitrile, to encapsulate your hands. You can avoid cross-contaminating the victims you treat by discarding, in a safe location, each pair of gloves when you move from person to person. Wear eye protection. If you have one available, wear a medical mask or respirator.

There are three types of bleeding:

- **Arterial bleeding.** Arteries transport blood under high pressure. Blood coming from an artery will spurt.

- **Venous bleeding.** Veins transport blood under low pressure. Blood coming from a vein will flow.

- **Capillary bleeding.** Capillaries also carry blood under low pressure. Capillary bleeding is surface bleeding and will ooze.

BLEEDING CONTROL TREATMENT

For minor cuts, clean the wound with soap and warm water and then cover with a bandage or sterile dressing.

For major cuts, use direct pressure and elevation. Remove or cut any clothing from around the wound. Remove jewelry that is in close proximity and that could possibly become an issue if swelling occurs. Elevate the wound above the heart. Do you remember being in school and raising your hand? When the teacher didn't call on you and your arm was left up in the air for several minutes, it would start to tingle. Your heart was having a difficult time pumping blood against gravity. The same principle applies when elevating a cut. Thanks to gravity there is reduced blood flow and thus, less blood loss.

With a gloved hand, place a clean cloth or gauze over the cut and hold it firmly in place for at least 10 minutes. (This is a task that can be done by the patient. If he or she is capable, have them or another patient with minor wounds apply the direct pressure, freeing you up to treat other patients.) Direct pressure holds platelets in place, allowing the blood to form a clot.

You can apply a "pressure bandage," which is a bandage tied around the affected area, to hold pressure for you. A pressure bandage should be tied in a bow that will allow you to easily and quickly loosen it when necessary.

Some patients can feel nauseous or light-headed when experiencing blood loss. If they experience these symptoms, lay them down and elevate their feet slightly. This will help prevent shock.

TOURNIQUETS

At one time it was taught that the next step to stop uncontrolled bleeding was to apply a tourniquet. A tourniquet is a band wrapped tightly to control severe bleeding. They are used on arm or leg injuries and have been reserved as a last resort to control blood loss. A tourniquet, when applied correctly, does in fact stop the bleeding, but may also cause severe tissue damage.

There are documented cases of amputations needed as a direct result of the application of a tourniquet. It is a dangerous maneuver that can have negative consequences. The debate continues, though: life over limb. Is it better to potentially lose an arm than to go into hypovolemic shock (an emergency condition in which, due to severe blood loss, the heart is unable to pump oxygenated blood to vital parts of the body) and possibly die? Many factors are involved and cases argued both for and against the use of a tourniquet.

In 2007 a gunman shot and killed 32 people and wounded 17 others on the campus of Virginia Tech University. Kevin Sterne was one of the injured, taking a bullet through the femoral artery of his right leg. Sterne used an electrical cord as makeshift tourniquet, which controlled the massive blood loss, and is said to have saved his own life.

The biggest issue with tourniquets is the difficulty of proper application. The band must be the correct width, placed in the right location, and tightened to the proper pressure. The bottom line is unless you have advanced training in the correct application of a tourniquet, you should avoid using them. Control bleeding with direct pressure and elevation.

SHOCK

The term "shock" can refer to wide range of medical conditions. It means and looks like different things to different people. One important thing to keep in mind is that shock is not an actual diagnosis. It is a symptom of a bigger problem that requires medical attention as soon as possible. Shock can be caused by numerous things, such as an allergic reaction, blood loss, or severe infection. Basically, it occurs when, for whatever reason, blood flow or blood volume is not sufficient to meet the needs of the body.

Shock Recognition

Early Stages

- Cool/sweaty skin

- Rapid pulse

- Anxiety

Late Stages

- Weakness/dizziness

- Nausea/vomiting

- Rapid/shallow breathing

- Confusion

- Thirst

- Weakening pulse

- Cyanosis (blue around the lips and fingers)

- Loss of consciousness

Shock Treatment

- Lay the victim supine (on their back)

- Evaluate their ABCs

- Control bleeding if necessary

- Elevate the feet 6 to 12 inches

- Loosen clothing

- Provide cooling or warmth to make the victim comfortable

- Seek professional medical care as soon as possible

BURNS

Burns are caused by heat, chemicals, electricity, friction, and radiation and they are divided into three categories. The degree of the burn is determined by the depth of the damage to the skin. The skin is the body's greatest defense against infection. Burns damage and compromise the skin, which can lead not only to infection but dehydration and possibly even hypothermia. The main goals for treating a burn are to stop the burning process, prevent shock, prevent infection, and ease pain. By determining the degree of a burn, you can determine the type of care needed.

FIRST-DEGREE BURNS

First-degree burns are superficial and typically cause redness and pain to the outer layer of the skin, or the epidermis. They usually heal with minimal treatment.

First-Degree Burn Recognition:
- Redness of the skin
- Swelling
- Pain

First-Degree Burn Treatment:
- Cool the burned area with running water or a cold compress.
- Apply topical burn ointment.
- Cover and protect the burned area with a sterile gauze bandage.
- Administer over-the-counter pain medication.

SECOND-DEGREE BURNS

Second-degree burns are slightly deeper into the second layer of skin, or dermis, and cause significant pain and blistering. They may require advanced medical care if and when it becomes available.

Second-Degree Burn Recognition:
- Skin is a deep red and splotchy

- Significant pain and swelling
- Blisters

Second-Degree Burn Treatment:
- If the burn is small (less than 3 inches in diameter) and not located on the face, groin, hands, feet, or on a major joint, treat as a first-degree burn.
- If the burn covers a large surface area or is located on one of the above-mentioned critical areas, treat as a third-degree burn.

THIRD-DEGREE BURNS

Also referred to as full-thickness burns, these are the most serious burns, causing damage into the subcutaneous layers of skin and posing a significant health risk. Advanced care is critical in the case of a third-degree burn. The skin can be black and charred or possibly dry and white.

Third-Degree Burn Recognition:
- Dry and leathery skin
- Skin may be black, white, brown, or yellow
- Swelling
- Pain may be absent due to the nerve endings being destroyed

Third-Degree Burn Treatment:
- Clean wound with sterile water and remove loose debris.
- Treat for shock.
- Do not remove burned clothing stuck to the wound.
- Cover the wound with loose sterile cloth.
- Elevate the wound if possible.
- If burns are to the face, check for breathing complications.
- DO NOT apply ointment, cream, ice, fluffy wound dressing, or medications to the wound.

CHEMICAL BURNS

Chemical burns can take place at home, work, or anywhere chemicals are stored or used, which is basically everywhere. They most often occur by accident, but sadly, they can happen by intent as well. Often, a commonly used product such as drain cleaner, paint thinner, or any one of a variety of other corrosive substances comes in contact with the skin. It is frequently identified by a leaking container or ruptured tank.

Chemical Burn Recognition:

- Redness, irritation, or burning at the site of contact
- Pain or numbness at the site of contact
- Blisters or charred skin at the site of contact
- Shortness of breath if fumes have been inhaled
- Weakness or dizziness
- Muscle twitching or seizures
- Cardiac arrest or irregular heartbeat

Chemical Burn Treatment:

- For a dry chemical, brush it off while wearing full PPE.
- Flush with water for several minutes. (Be aware that some chemicals have adverse reactions to water, so obtain as much knowledge as you can about the chemical before flushing.)
- Cover with sterile dressing.
- Seek professional medical care as soon as possible.
- Do not apply ice or puncture blisters.

MEDICAL EMERGENCIES

Among the fractured limbs, blood-soaked clothing, and other forms of trauma associated with catastrophic events are medical emergencies. They are often the quiet killers that go undetected among the chaos. Heart attacks, diabetic emergencies, seizures, and allergic reactions are sprinkled among the injured. All too often, the most vocal victims or visually alarming injuries receive the attention while others quietly suffer from a potentially deadly medical emergency.

Regardless of the medical emergency, the most important thing you can do is to identify what may be happening, take whatever steps you can to ensure their ABCs, and get them to a medical facility as soon as possible. Often, the required treatment is advanced medical care that cannot be performed in makeshift treatment areas staffed by volunteer rescuers. There's little that you can do "in the field" to correct the problem. Victims often know the history of their diagnosed medical problems. Ask them. If they don't know or are unable to answer your questions, you should be able to recognize some of the more common conditions. Below are four medical emergencies and common ways you can identify them.

HEART ATTACKS

A "heart attack" is technically known as a myocardial infarction. "Myo" means muscle, "cardial" means the heart, and "infarction" is the death of tissue due to lack of blood supply. During a heart attack, oxygenated blood cannot be circulated to the vital organs of the body. Heart muscle requires a constant supply of oxygen-rich blood and any lapse causes pain and the death of heart muscle. The following are symptoms of a heart attack:

- Chest pain
- Shortness of breath
- Nausea
- Pain in arms, back, neck, or jaw
- A history of high blood pressure or other cardiac conditions

Field treatment: Calm the patient and give them medical oxygen if you have it available. If they are conscious enough to maintain their own airway and are able to tolerate aspirin (some cannot due to side effects), give them some to help relieve chest pain. Transport them to a medical facility as soon as possible.

COLD WEATHER-RELATED EMERGENCIES

When the terms frostbite and hypothermia are used, scenes of blinding snowfall and subzero temperatures immediately come to mind. While these situations certainly are the cause of many cold weather-related medical emergencies, such conditions don't always have to be the case for problems to arise. The human body, extremely durable in many categories, can be extremely temperamental when it comes to temperature. When the body's core temperature drops below 98.6°F, the risk for temperature-related medical issues begins to rise. As the core temperature drops, the risk for hypothermia increases. Hypothermia occurs when the body's temperature continues to drop below what it requires for normal function, which by definition, is 95°F.

Hypothermia often begins with physiological responses to maintain and preserve heat, such as shivering and elevated heart rate and blood pressure. Later signs include loss of coordination, confusion, and cyanosis (bluish discoloration) around the ears, lips, fingers, and toes. As hypothermia sets in to severe stages, the person may become severely confused and combative. The skin becomes blue and puffy. Eventually, organs will fail and death can occur.

Field treatment: Move the victim to a warm environment. Remove any wet clothing. Begin active rewarming by placing the victim under loose, dry layers and rubbing the skin.

If the victim can support their own airway (able to breathe and speak), have them drink warm beverages. Avoid having them drink alcohol as it is counterproductive to the body's natural processes. Alcohol increases blood flow to the skin, giving the person the feeling of warmth when in all actuality the body's temperature could be continuing to decrease.

If frostbite is suspected (grayish or white waxy skin and numbness are present), protect the affected area, but do not rub the skin. Body heat can be used to passively warm the affected area. You can use your own body heat to warm that of the victim. The warmest areas of the body are the armpit and the groin. Do not actively warm the person by, for example, laying them next to a campfire, because the skin is numb and at risk of burning.

If hypothermia is suspected, do not immerse the victim in warm water; it can cause irregular and dangerous heart activity. Instead, warm the person with layers of warm, dry blankets and, if possible, use the body heat of another person.

In any case of suspected frostbite or hypothermia, get the victim to a hospital as quickly as possible.

DIABETIC EMERGENCY

Hypoglycemia (low blood sugar) is often the cause of diabetic emergencies. Giving the patient food or glucose will often remedy the problem. Another condition, hyperglycemia (high blood sugar) cannot be as easily rectified. Giving a hyperglycemic patient sugar is not typically problematic and will not cause their condition to worsen, so offering a diabetic patient with a patent airway food is never wrong. The following symptoms can be indicative of hypo- or hyperglycemia:

- Dizziness or lightheadedness
- Mental instability
- Excessive hunger, urination, or thirst
- Ketoacidosis (extremely serious condition marked by fruity breath, dry skin, and vomiting)

Field treatment: If the patient is a known diabetic and can support their own airway, have them consume something with sugar in it, preferably in liquid form at first. Juice, soda, or water mixed with sugar is a quick and easy way to raise their level of blood sugar. Remember, diet soda has no sugar. That should be followed up with something more substantial such as a peanut butter and jelly sandwich, or even candy. Their condition should improve within minutes. If it does not, or if they are unresponsive, transport them to a medical facility as soon as possible.

SEIZURE

A seizure is an interruption of electrical activity in the brain. These abnormal signals from the brain cause the body to convulse or seize. The cause can vary from person to person. Someone can be prone to seizures due to a seizure disorder such as epilepsy. They can occur when the body's core temperature quickly elevates. Low blood sugar can cause a seizure, as can a variety of other reasons. During a seizure the body will shake (either violently or mildly) for a short period of time, usually a minute or two. Then the person will go into a postictal state, which is an altered level of consciousness that occurs in between the seizure and normal baseline status. The patient can appear to be asleep or will stare off into space, usually for about 5 to 10 minutes. Look out for the following symptoms:

- Collapse accompanied by violent shaking
- A fixed stare
- Unresponsiveness

Field treatment: The best thing that you can do is to keep the person from hurting him or herself and allow the seizure to happen. Lay the person down, loosen any clothing around their neck, and clear objects away that may injure them. Once the person has finished seizing and is in a postictal state, roll them onto their side in the "recovery position" to help maintain an open airway and prevent suffocation. The postictal state will last anywhere from 5 to 30 minutes, during which they will slowly recover and regain their ability to speak and move.

ALLERGIC REACTION

An allergic reaction occurs when the body identifies something as a threat. It begins to fight the substance (which is many times harmless, such as medication, pollen, dust mites, food, etc.). The body's reaction can result in minor issues (rash, itchy eyes, runny nose) or a more severe reaction (difficulty breathing or nausea). There are many types of allergies: seasonal, food, medicinal, animal, latex, etc. An allergic reaction is not necessarily a medical emergency, but a severe reaction, known as anaphylaxis, can be extremely dangerous. Take caution when the following symptoms arise:

- Skin irritation (redness, itching, swelling, etc.)
- Anxiety
- Wheezing or shortness of breath

- Stuffy or runny nose
- Bloodshot, itchy, or watery eyes
- Nausea, vomiting, or diarrhea
- Swollen lips, tongue, or throat

Field treatment: There is no way to predict how severe the reaction will become, at which time advanced medical care is needed. A slight allergic reaction can be remedied with an over-the-counter antihistamine such as Benadryl. Many times people with a known severe allergy will carry epinephrine or an EpiPen. An EpiPen is a self-administered, measured-dose medication that can be injected in the case of an anaphylactic reaction. Those who carry one should be familiar with it and can usually tell you how to administer it. Although, in cases of anaphylaxis, they may not be able to, in which case, simply follow the instructions printed on the label. Prescriptions can vary from person to person so you should avoid administering an EpiPen to anyone but the person to whom it was prescribed.

SUMMARY

Disaster medical operations are aimed particularly at triage and trauma. The greatest medical results stem from accurately sorting and treating the most severely injured first. There are three phases of trauma:

Phase 1. Death within minutes as a result of overwhelming and irreversible damage to vital organs.

Phase 2. Death within several hours as a result of excessive bleeding.

QUICK FIRST AID EXTRAS

Nosebleed. Have the bleeding person pinch their nose, breath through their mouth, and lean forward until bleeding has stopped.

Animal bite. Immediately flush the wound with water. Then, wash the wound thoroughly with soap and water and seek medical attention as soon as possible.

Eye injury. Do not allow the patient to rub their eye. Flush the eye with copious amounts of water. If you can see the object, try to remove it carefully with a clean cloth.

Splinter. Most visible splinters can be removed with simple tweezers. If the length of the splinter is under the skin, use a sterilized needle to slit the skin over the splinter and then tweezers to remove it. Clean the wound and apply an antibiotic ointment.

Phase 3. Death within several days or weeks as a result of infection or organ failure. Many disaster victims in the second or third phase can be saved by simple medical care.

Even though CPR is not often performed in a mass casualty situation, you should take an American Heart Association class and obtain your CPR certification, as well as take a variety of first aid courses available in your area. One can never receive enough training or preparation, particularly in the area of first aid. Lives matter most as disaster recovery begins. Any advanced knowledge or preparation you can obtain could reap many benefits when the need arises in your community. When it does arise, you can take what you've learned here and the additional training you have received and make a positive difference. Wear proper PPE to keep yourself protected and then do the greatest good for the greatest number of people.

CHAPTER 7
DISASTER PSYCHOLOGY

This book repetitively preaches the importance of personal protective equipment. Ensuring your own safety is an absolute necessity so that you can provide care for those that need you. Gloves, a mask, and a helmet all help to keep you protected. One area, unfortunately, is vulnerable regardless of how well you protect yourself: your psychological health.

In the past few decades, numerous large-scale disasters have brought substantial attention to the long-term effects of traumatic situations on the population, particularly in the area of mental health. Death, destruction, fear, and loss all have consequences. Often overlooked are the contamination of good mental health and physical well-being. The connection between the state of mental health and physical well-being is a strong one. The two are closely related and can greatly affect one another.

Generally speaking, the majority of people are bystanders to disaster. It is seen in movies, read about it in books, and watched in glimpses flashing across our television screens on the news. Those experiences are mere snapshots of the immense and overwhelming reality of what is actually happening. It is when we are directly affected that the mental and sometimes physical toll is taken.

January 21, 2005, was a typical day at the fire station for me. I checked my equipment in, poured a cup of coffee, and began doing station duties just as I do every other day at work. Over the loudspeaker at my station, emergency calls are dispatched for the entire county all day long and, having been a firefighter for several years, I have acquired the skill of tuning out most of the chatter unless it directly affects me. That morning something caught my attention. The dispatcher's voice reported an "aircraft emergency." Even though the city where I work has a population of over 180,000 people and covers 75 square miles, we are a suburban department and typically don't have many occurrences of aircraft emergencies.

Shortly after takeoff, a Cessna 421C with five people on board had somehow crashed into the back of a home in the middle of a neighborhood. My fire engine was not called on the initial alarm, but was called in to relieve crews that were. As we arrived on the scene, we were advised that there were no survivors. Five of us were assigned to assist the coroner in recovering human remains so that he could positively identify the five people.

For over eight hours that cold January day we had the gruesome task of collecting the scattered remains of the five people who boarded that plane hours before. Firefighters are no strangers to death. We deal with it on an almost-daily basis. This was different. At the end of the day, Battalion Chief Mark Messinger began making conversation with me. At least, I thought it was conversation. Chief Messinger had been trained in Critical Incident Stress Management (CISM) and was actually interrogating me. Our conversation concluded by him sending me and two other firefighters home for the remainder of the shift.

At first I was confused and maybe a little bit irritated at being sent home. I saw it as a sign of weakness. Death, even tragic death, is just a part of the job. I'm a firefighter. I can handle this, I thought. He saw something that I hadn't. When we cleared the call and returned to the station, I reluctantly removed my gear from the rig and went home for the night. I brushed it off as being no big deal, but if I were to be honest with myself, I was feeling physically and mentally exhausted. I went to bed that night with a constant replay of the feelings, sights, sounds, and smells of the day. When I woke up the next morning they were right there. Vivid images flashed through my mind and continued to do so for days, even weeks after. Every one of my senses was continually replaying that day. I was reluctantly consumed.

Chief Messinger was right. I was in no mental condition to be able to respond to other emergency calls the night of the crash. I was distracted, which is dangerous in my profession. He saw visual and verbal clues and was able to identify that I was having critical incident stress issues and he managed it by relieving me of my duty for the day. I later thanked him because I didn't know it at the time, but I was hurting. Due to years of training and experience I was able to get the job done, but what I wasn't able to do was disguise the fact that my cup was full.

I've heard that traumatic events, even minor ones, are like an icon appearing on your computer desktop. Eventually, that desktop will be full. It may not be the most tragic event or worst thing you've experienced, but there will be one situation that pushes you over that line. Your emotional cup is full and even the addition of the tiniest drop causes it to spill over.

PREPARING THE MIND TO ACT

Most people live their lives working and playing in areas where there are few consequences to action or inaction. Lives are simply lived. But when our world is turned upside-down in a moment of crisis, our brains begin to work differently. We've seen the movies and think we have an understanding of how we would react if the proverbial excrement were to hit the fan. But we don't. Emotion and stress overtake logic and reason. The ability of perception begins to erode and we miss visual and verbal cues around us.

In the classic movie *Cool Hand Luke,* the main character, played by Paul Newman, tries to adjust to prison life, without much success. He is told that he needs to get his "mind right." By aligning your mind with your circumstances you are better able to make good decisions. This is true for all aspects of life, whether you are trying to lose weight, quit smoking, learn a language, or prepare for disaster. No one can or should be able to mentally prepare for the atrocities you may encounter in a disaster, but you should expect the worst. In order to achieve the best possible outcome under the worst possible circumstances, you not only need to prepare supplies, but you to get your "mind right."

You can prepare your mind by recognizing your role during and following a disastrous event. That role is going to be physically, mentally, and emotionally demanding. By understanding that beforehand, you will be able to better manage your actions and decisions in the time of crisis. The most powerful muscle in the body is the brain. It is possible to actually utilize your brain to exceed physical limitations. Mind over matter. Your body can be pushed beyond what you think you are physically capable of doing. There are several techniques often used in the military and athletics to do so. Just as going to the gym trains your body, you can train your brain with mental preparedness exercises.

The Navy SEALs teach a visualization technique they call emergency conditioning. It refers to the act of acclimating your brain to the demands placed on your mind and body in battle. The same technique can be applied to disaster preparation. Envision the worst-case scenarios before they happen—the sights, sounds, smells, exhaustion, and fear. If you can envision something in vivid detail, your brain creates a bookmark very similar to an actual experience.

As you become proficient in emergency conditioning, your brain will refer back to the previous "experiences" that are on file. Then, during the actual crisis, when a quick decision or action is required, that decision is made by the brain tapping into a system of "experience files." It searches for those previous experiences recalling how you reacted to them before, good or bad, and the associated feelings. Unbeknownst to you, your brain then determines your "gut feelings" and reactions. Those memories that you fabricated have dictated your behavior in a critical situation.

To get your mind right, you must consciously force yourself to face reality. Something bad has just happened and you are going to need to control your sensibilities. Survivors or heroes aren't immune to fear. Fear is a normal and healthy function of the body. They experience fear just as everyone else, but are able to manage it. They acknowledge what has happened and are able to look ahead and consider "what do I do next."

RESPONSE OF THE BODY AND MIND TO DISASTER

Stress and fear create certain behaviors that prevent reason and logical thinking. But the result isn't always negative. You've undoubtedly heard the story of the mom who was able to lift a car off of her trapped child. No one knows how the car ended up on the child or if this "woman" or "child" actually exist, yet everyone seemingly knows the story of the heroic and maternal mom who was able to lift a car up and save her child's life. It is likely a parable and a testament to mothers caring for their offspring. But, there is actually science behind such a scenario. When you are "altered" by fear and stress, perception, cognition, and memory become impaired, but chemicals race through the body that cause it to be in a heightened state of readiness. Blood changes chemistry so that it is better able to coagulate and muscle tone alters. Survival instincts engage. The body readies itself for confrontation.

After the event, body chemistry returns to normal. What remains are the psychological processes that can heal the mental wounds or can sometimes lie hidden, festering below the surface, eroding mental well-being. Initially it is easy for rescuers to become emotionally overwhelmed. Large-scale destruction, mass casualties, or even individualized trauma can emotionally damage even the toughest among us. Rescuers may cry or shout out against God, Mother Nature, terrorists, or whomever they feel is responsible. They empathize with victims and personalize their injuries or death. Do not mistake this for an emotional flaw or weakness. It is a normal reaction and part of natural psychological process.

Take caution not to over-identify with victims and assume their feelings. It will only hamper your ability to do your job and could have potential long-term mental affects. Avoid taking ownership of another's problems. During disaster recovery, it is common for rescuers to experience compassion fatigue, also known as secondary victimization. The victim's feelings, both physical and emotional, begin to manifest themselves in the rescuer. It is an insidious process that may produce disassociation, anxiety, sleep disturbances, nightmares, or an overall feeling of powerlessness.

EFFECTS OF TRAUMATIC STRESS

The effects of traumatic stress vary from person to person, but some responses are prevalent among survivors. An overwhelming loss of faith in safety, predictability, and meaning in life occurs frequently. "Normalcy" has been shattered and everything seems uncertain. Logic is overrun by stress and emotion. Traumatic events are processed differently in the brain than other events are, often preventing the survivor from returning to normal life without sometimes debilitating side effects.

Traumatic stress may affect cognitive functioning. Decision making becomes difficult. A survivor may act out irrationally in ways that are out of character. Curious memory gaps involving day-to-day events, known as dissociative amnesia, may develop. Basic behaviors can be altered to the point where others might say, "they're just not themselves."

Physical health can be affected as well. Blood flow to the brain surges under traumatic stress and can lead to sustained high blood pressure. Often, as a coping mechanism or a form of emotional escape, a survivor may turn to alcohol or drug use. Depression and lethargy create a propensity for obesity and tobacco use. Energy levels often decrease. Multiple medical conditions are also tied to post-traumatic stress, such as dementia, chronic pain, autoimmune disease, irritable bowel syndrome, and liver disease. Physical health and mental health are closely related and caring for one should not mean neglecting the other.

Interpersonal relationships often suffer after a stressful incident. Those who survive may experience short- or long-term changes in their personality. Fits of anger or unreasonable rage that occur become dangerous for the affected person as well as those closest to him or her. There may be flashbacks or visions that a survivor will go to great lengths to avoid. Again, alcohol and drug abuse take their toll. Sometimes, someone who has experienced psychological trauma can become unusually dependent on partners, family members, and friends. That can translate to emotional or financial dependency, as well as other forms. Interest in sexual activity or social activities decreases as their penchant for isolation increases. So, not only does traumatic stress affect the survivor, it bleeds over and touches all those around them.

POST-TRAUMATIC STRESS DISORDER

In 1980 the American Psychiatric Association added post-traumatic stress disorder (PTSD) to its mental disorder classification scheme, thus making it a legitimate diagnosis. Though often attributed to military personnel, the study of PTSD has been found to affect those who have sustained natural disasters, mass casualty events, or personal mental trauma.

Survivors of a crisis experience a wide range of mental and physiological reactions. One person's reaction can be vastly different from that of someone else who encountered the same circumstances. While one person may repeatedly break down and cry, feeling withdrawn from their normal life because of a traumatic experience, someone else might feel they have been given a second chance by overcoming the trauma, making positive life choices afterward. These separate reactions are dependent on a variety of factors, which include the scale of the disaster, prior experiences, and emotional strength.

Just as you look for signs and symptoms of injury in the survivors of the event, also be aware of signs and symptoms in fellow rescuers. Keep an eye on each other and look for any change in behavior or physical health. Specific symptoms, both psychological and physical, are associated with trauma.

Physical Symptoms of Trauma

- Chest pain
- Diarrhea
- Fatigue

- Headache
- Hyperactivity
- Loss of appetite
- Nightmares
- Sleep disturbances
- Stomach pain or nausea

Psychological Symptoms of Trauma

- Fear of reoccurrence
- Feelings of helplessness
- Inability to concentrate
- Increased alcohol or drug consumption
- Irritability
- Isolation or withdrawal
- Mood swings
- Numbness
- Relationship strife
- Sadness or depression
- Self-blame

A self-defense mechanism that emergency responders often use is a form of emotional separation. You can't allow yourself to think about the body lying without a heartbeat in front of you as a person with family, a career, fears, and dreams. It is a job to be done. You follow protocols. You do what you are trained to do. You secure the airway, breathe for them, perform compressions, push medications, and analyze their heart rhythm. On that cloudy, frigid day in January I spent hours among the remains of five people that woke up that morning expecting to be on the beach that night. Over time, standing in the wreckage, I had inadvertently lost the ability to separate. I personalized every single one of them. I became withdrawn, irritable, and numb. I didn't recognize it in myself. I thought those feelings were safely under my exterior facade as they always had been. It took the awareness of a fellow responder to identify that I wasn't well.

Fortunately my symptoms eased over time. But it is common for them to persist or worsen. Victims of PTSD often believe there will be no end to their feelings. People will display different aspects of unprocessed emotions as they try to make sense of what happened. Often there is a perpetual sense of depression and painful memories. Studies have shown that human-inflicted trauma, as opposed to an "act-of-God" event, tends to be more traumatic for the survivors. The more extreme and prolonged the event, the greater the chances for PTSD. This is why post-traumatic stress disorder is so prevalent in the military, where soldiers are subjected to sustained times of anxiety, a direct and continued threat to their life, and exposure to death.

Reducing PTSD does not mean fighting the symptoms, but working with the feelings. The symptoms are an indication of an underlying issue. Make the rescue operation more responsive to victims' and rescuers' psychological needs. As long as it does not interfere with rescue activities, encourage those involved to express their feelings to help avoid "emotional overload." Both mental and physical benefits result from engaging in open and honest conversation.

To help relieve rescuers of disaster-related stress you should brief personnel on what to expect to see and feel as they conduct their operations; emphasize teamwork to ease the workload and diffuse emotional overload; rotate personnel; ensure proper hydration and nutrition; and encourage breaks. These steps won't eliminate all the effects of PTSD, but may mitigate some of the long-term effects before they begin.

PTSD IN CHILDREN

Children, just as adults, can experience post-traumatic stress disorder from a variety of causes. There are millions of reported cases of PTSD in children who suffer from abuse, neglect, and disaster survival. Children are just as susceptible as adults to post-traumatic stress following a natural or man-made disaster. In some cases, they are even more so. One factor for children that does not necessarily affect adults is the correlation between experiencing stress symptoms and seeing how their parents react to the traumatic event. Adults aren't as likely to mirror someone else's feelings as children, who will look to adults to see how to react or feel. Children tend to be less affected if they have strong family support and parents who weren't greatly affected.

Rather than experiencing flashbacks the way that many adults do, children, particularly those under the age of 12, seem to remember events in the wrong order. They also tend to remember events leading up to the trauma as a potential cause, thus thinking that by avoiding those events in the future they can avoid the associated traumatic event. They also can show evidence of PTSD in the way they play. For example, if they were to experience a school shooting, grade school children will sometimes play shooting games or even bring a firearm to school.

One difference between teenage children and younger children is the tendency for behavioral issues. Teenagers tend to become really introverted, impulsive, or aggressive in behavior. Self-harm becomes a concern with teenage children and they will be in "trouble" more as they struggle to cope with and process what has happened.

Once again showing their resilience, children often return to normal behavior after a few months. Counseling is typically recommended to help the process along. If the symptoms persist there are many options for seeking help, but the most important thing is to recognize the PTSD and get them the help they need as soon as possible.

CRITICAL INCIDENT STRESS MANAGEMENT

Critical Incident Stress Management (CISM) is an intervention protocol developed for dealing with traumatic events. It is most commonly used with firefighters, police officers, military personnel, medical workers, and air traffic controllers, but its usage has expanded to meet the needs of anyone who has experienced a traumatic event. It is a formalized process for dealing with the aftereffects of psychological trauma. It is not psychotherapy, although it has been referred to as "psychological first aid."

As with most things in disaster recovery, CISM has its origins in the military. It was first identified as "combat stress" during the Civil War, when soldiers were ridiculed and even imprisoned for showing signs of psychological stress associated with battle. It was viewed as a sign of mental weakness. In the following years, intervention techniques were developed to overcome war-related stress and eventually used to treat symptoms from a variety of stressful situations.

Most survivors experience a particular process when dealing with the aftermath of a crisis. Mental health professionals have identified the four emotional phases of crisis.

- **The Impact Phase.** The event has happened and survivors take care of themselves and their families. They may not panic and show little or no emotion.

- **The Inventory Phase.** Survivors assess what has happened and take inventory of who and what is left. They may try to locate other survivors. During this phase traditional social ties tend to be discarded in favor of more practical and functional relationships that are required at the time because of the disaster.

- **The Rescue Phase.** A kinship and bond form between survivors as they seek out fellow victims and conduct search-and-rescue operations. Survivors are often very helpful and compliant during this phase.

- **The Recovery Phase.** Emotional stressors begin to add up. In the recovery phase, people may feel that rescue operations are not happening quickly enough or in the most efficient way possible and can actually pull together *against* rescuers.

Various processes take place when conducting critical incident stress management. The primary and most common components involve a defusing (also called a "hot wash"), a debriefing, and then follow-up. CISM sessions are voluntary and confidential. Because of the severe emotional implications, they are preferably conducted by someone officially trained in stress management. The following are the steps that happen during a CISM session:

Defusing. A hot wash usually happens at or near the scene immediately after the event has been mitigated. The main purpose is to stabilize people affected by the incident so they can return to their normal routines. It is not a critique of the event but a forum to discuss what happened and the resulting feelings.

1. Establish rapport. Talk with the victims and encourage them to talk about their feelings as well as their psychological needs.

2. Listen. Take the time to listen and offer your undivided attention.

3. Empathize. Do not say, "I know how you feel," or relate your own stories. Simply let them know that it's OK for them to feel that way.

4. Provide confidentiality. Respect their confidence and do not repeat personal information.

Debriefing. This is a formalized group discussion about a particularly distressing critical incident and is usually conducted 24 to 72 hours after the event. There are seven steps to a debriefing. Like the defusing, a debriefing is not a critique.

1. Pre-debriefing. Gather relevant information and identify any specific needs of the group before the debriefing process begins. Ensure that you yourself are up to performing the debriefing.

2. Contact/contract. Introduce yourself and inquire as to what the group's expectation of the debriefing is.

3. Story. Ask open-ended questions about the event to help them explore their thoughts, facts, and sensory experiences around it. Examples of questions are: What happened next? What did it look like? What were you thinking at the time?

4. Impact. Focus on feelings rather than facts. This can be the most emotionally difficult part of the debriefing. Examples of questions are: What was the hardest part for you? What were you feeling at that time?

5. Symptom education. This is the opportunity to assist the survivor in understanding their symptoms. Help to identify and normalize the feelings for them. This is where advanced training in CISM is essential.

6. Current functioning and coping. Create a coping plan that includes stress management techniques, developing goals, and setting up a support system.

7. Follow-up. Determine if there is anything else they would like to talk about. Often participants are asked to verbalize one thing they are going to do to take care of themselves. Identify their needs and point them to sources of additional assistance. Participants are encouraged to support one another and to expect reactions for the following days and weeks. Set up follow-up time if needed or just informally check on them in a few days.

SUMMARY

An important part of managing a crisis is ensuring the well-being of fellow rescuers. While large-scale events like natural disasters, terrorist attacks, and civil unrest are on the rise, fortunately they don't happen often enough for most people to have any level of proficiency at managing them, which emphasizes the importance of being mentally and physically ready. Preparedness and training will reduce overall stress both during and after the event.

Statistically, the number of people who sustain long-term affects created by traumatic stress is low. Though they don't forget, the majority of people find ways to cope and go on about their lives with some sort of regularity. By normalizing common reactions and maintaining an awareness of coping mechanisms, you will be better able to reduce long-term severe reactions.

A few days after the plane crash in 2005, I attended a critical incident stress management debriefing. Attendance was optional to all emergency responders who were present the day of the crash. I discounted the importance and told people that I was going to attend just to see what it was like. After all, I had been a part of dozens of traumatic and devastating responses in my career; this one seemed only marginally different. Nearly every fireman, paramedic, and police officer who responded to the crash showed up that day. It was a full room of people who had never experienced an official debriefing but were searching for something. Maybe because of the magnitude of what we had seen and done that day or because the cumulative years of trauma that we experience regularly had taken their toll, I saw experienced hardened men who are true heroes break down and cry.

Because we were professionally trained, somewhat mentally prepared, and received quality follow-up CISM, I'm unaware of any long-term effects plaguing any of the responders. Everyone got right back up on those trucks, ambulances, and police cars and went back to work. Just as important as preparing your home and supplies for disaster, so is preparing your mental condition. Disaster can reach out and touch anyone. Studies have linked the strength of one's mental health to their physical health and quality of life. Prepare yourself beforehand and provide opportunities for psychological treatment and care afterward.

Every time I drive by the neighborhood where it happened, I immediately go back to that plane crash and can still recall with vivid detail what that scene looked like. Usually I'm in the car with my family and don't say a word—I just drive by and acknowledge that tragedy lurks around every corner and that mental and physical preparation before a crisis are just as important as attention to mental and physical well-being after the fact. Because I had those around me who cared enough to identify the signs and symptoms of critical incident stress, I'm better for it and got my "mind right."

CHAPTER 8

DISASTER PREPAREDNESS NETWORKS

In some ways working backward, this chapter will introduce concepts and terminology that come into play in areas covered by all the previous chapters. In essence, you've learned how to perform all the components of a disaster response, and now you will put the pieces together in an organized fashion. Amid the chaos of crisis, an astonishing amount of systematic organization occurs behind the scenes.

People will help people. That fact has been proven time and again throughout history. What is changing, though, is the desire to be prepared and organized. The past several decades have seen a growth in community emergency response groups constructed by like-minded individuals, factions of trained cohesive citizens. All over the country you will find examples of selfless individuals helping where they can, but also communities that have organized and responded as a united team.

In March of 2011, a dozen members of an Astoria, Oregon, community emergency response team came to the aid of its citizens by setting up a relocation shelter. A tsunami had been reported in the Pacific Ocean and while police and fire crews evacuated coastal areas, that 12-member team reported to a local elementary school where, with some guidance from local authorities, they prepared for an influx of emergency responders and relocated citizens who could potentially need food, shelter, and aid. They staffed the post overnight until the all-clear was given. Police and fire crews could not meet all the needs at the time and enlisted the help of organized and trained neighborhood response groups such as this one.

During the same tsunami threat, an organized neighborhood group of almost 40 people assisted local law enforcement by patrolling the beaches in Monterey, California. Under the direction of the police department, they helped to evacuate people further inland as well as offered updates on tidal conditions, which they received on their very high frequency (VHF) radios.

A Cameron, Missouri, group helped in the search for a missing woman. The sheriff's department utilized neighborhood response members to assist in the ground search. Police chief Corey Sloan stated, "The collaborative efforts of the Dekalb County Sheriff's Department, Missouri State Highway Patrol, Cameron Police and Fire departments and, most importantly, the Cameron CERT proved instrumental and most likely saved the life of this 82-year-old woman."

Lee County, Florida, neighborhood groups worked tirelessly to prepare its citizens for a tropical storm by answering informational phone lines, staffing shelters, and assisting emergency responders.

In the aftermath of a particularly harsh winter, North Dakota was being bombarded with widespread spring flooding. Neighborhood groups organized and worked countless hours performing a variety of tasks from sandbagging to relocating victims, assisting in shelters, and helping local governments document disaster operations.

There are numerous documented examples of neighborhood emergency response groups coming to the aid of their fellow citizens during tropical storms, building fires, missing person searches, flooding, wildfires, earthquakes, and blizzards. Emergency management personnel not only welcome your help for an imminent or unfolding crisis, they need it. Some cases of large-scale incidents involving local, state, and federal responders and smaller-scale neighborhood crises, such as an apartment complex fire, require local citizens to rally and ensure everyone is cared for. In either scenario, citizens are called upon to aid when a community is in need. Pre-event coordination will offer the best and most streamlined disaster response. This chapter will outline everything from constructing a community disaster response team to organizing meetings and mobilizing.

GETTING STARTED

Neighbor. It is a subjective word. To those who live in densely populated areas, a neighbor is often regarded as someone who geographically adjoins your property; the people living in the home or apartment on either side of you. In more rural areas, a neighbor can be someone who lives within a several-mile radius of your home or property. For the purposes of this book, your neighbor is anyone who will be in close proximity to you during a disaster. It could be the person next door, your coworker at the office, or the farmer a mile away.

Sadly, the majority of people will remain apathetic toward disaster preparedness until they experience one. Only a small percentage of the population will choose to participate in a disaster-response group prior to a crisis. But, by providing sound reasoning, good training, strategic planning, and educational materials, you may create much more buy-in for the unmotivated. They key to building a successful program is to establish an ongoing process that will continue to interest and challenge the core group of people in your community.

IDENTIFY PREEXISTING GROUPS IN YOUR COMMUNITY

Do some homework before organizing the people around you into a response group. Identify any existing groups in your immediate area. Oftentimes, particularly if you are new to an area, some semblance of organization is already in place. It could be as loose as a neighbor who has a lot of "stuff," where neighbors tend to gather to evaluate the damage and decide where help is needed, or as structured as a well-defined network and command system outlining who is in charge of what and who reports to where. It will save you a lot of work and effort if you can locate a functioning group and see where and how you can help. That will eliminate confusion as well as misunderstandings with local authorities and other emergency response groups.

If there are no current organized response groups to join, create one. Begin by making phone calls. There are several departments, groups, and organizations that you can call for three purposes: to help identify other response groups in your area, for information and literature to begin to organize your own, and for contact information for whom to call and how best to communicate with them during a disaster. A few examples are the local fire department, any local Office of Emergency Services, the Red Cross, the Salvation Army, and the Humane Society.

Your fire department is a good place to start since they are the primary player in any disaster response for almost every single municipality. The first to respond, organize, and coordinate with outside agencies, they will bring the most initial responders and apparatus to the disaster site. Having aided in events ranging from single-unit responses to incidents that tax every resource in the region, I can tell you that, at least initially, your fire department will be coordinating search, rescue, and medical operations.

Fire departments will often have a public relations representative or a designated firefighter who can answer any questions you may have or offer advice for what you will need to organize a response group in your community. When you call the fire department or the local offices mentioned above, ask specific questions like the following:

- Is there someone I can speak with regarding neighborhood disaster organization and response?

- Does the fire department already have a plan in place that includes organizing neighborhoods? If so, tell me about it. If not, would they be interested in helping me organize my neighborhood to better assist during a crisis?

- Are there any other organized neighborhood disaster response groups in the area? If so, how can I contact them?

- Does the fire department have a representative who would be willing to participate in my neighborhood meeting to offer information and guidance?

- Does the fire department offer disaster training of any kind? If so, what? When? Where? And how much? If not, where would you recommend we receive training?

- Are there training materials available to the public, such as books, pamphlets, or videos?

Fire, police, and emergency medical services (EMS) are becoming more progressive as they realize that, when done correctly, neighborhood response teams can be a valuable asset and professional responders should cooperate and be involved with their organization and training.

The Humane Society was included in this list for the sole purpose of rescuing and safeguarding pets during a disaster. Missing pets cause stress and worry in what is already an extremely trying time. Displaced pets can also create a dangerous situation. They can be scared and confused, which can create aggressive behavior. Locate your local Humane Society and include any assistance they can offer in your disaster planning. There are questions you will want to ask them as well.

- Does the Humane Society have a disaster plan in place for animals?

- Is there a representative from the Humane Society that would be an emergency contact and that could offer information to my neighborhood response group?

- Would that representative be willing to come to a meeting to speak to our group and answer questions?

- Is there any additional training that you offer or would recommend to help with animal rescue during a disaster?

ORGANIZE A GROUP OF LIKE-MINDED INDIVIDUALS

Next, ask around to see if there are any neighborhood functions where you can test the waters and begin the conversation with those around you about the need for organization during a disaster. If there are others who also recognize the need, or even if they seem ambivalent about it, get their contact information and tell them your thoughts and plans. Begin with your closest neighbors and the people you already know. You should not be aggressively pursuing participants, "aggressively" being the operative word. This runs the risk of your quickly becoming labeled as paranoid or Chicken Little ("The sky is falling!"). Rather, state your concerns about what could be done and how you would like to help. Chances are there are many around you with the same concerns and the same desire to help. Anticipate cultural, ethnic, religious, and other forms of diversity in your neighborhood. Be aware of the differences and understand the character of your neighborhood and its people. Be respectful.

CONSTRUCT A COMMUNITY DISASTER RESPONSE TEAM

By understanding your area's inherent disasters, you can better focus your efforts on what you are most likely to face. Some regions are prone to flooding, while others are threatened by tornados or earthquakes. Your efforts should not be singular, though. Some places could potentially face a variety of disasters, sometimes simultaneously. California, for example, encounters earthquakes, wildfires, tsunamis, mudslides, and flooding. While certain threats can be emphasized, overall readiness is the end goal. With information in hand, you can begin to organize people, data, supplies, and strategies.

Make no mistake, organizing and maintaining a community response group takes work. Take care of a few things prior to your first meeting. It is sometimes beneficial to enlist a few others who have the same desire as you to prepare your community. Talk to a few friends and neighbors about what you would like to do and why. Just because you have the desire for a coordinated disaster response group in your community does not mean that you have to be the leader. Every individual has certain strengths and weaknesses. Your strength may not be in a role of leadership. Even if it is not your intention to be the "leader" of the group, it IS your role to excite a few others about the prospect of organization and share the concept with those around you.

Once you have identified a few others with a common vision, you have what is referred to as a "start-up team" or a "steering committee." Use your small group to determine large needs. Together you have three main objectives: establish goals, determine the boundaries of your neighborhood, and organize the first meeting.

Establish goals. Your goals should reflect the specific needs of the neighborhood and surrounding communities. Your goals should be SMART: specific, measurable, attainable, relevant, and time-bound. Keeping the end result in mind, the goals should be for the initial set-up of your group.

Determine boundaries. The easy way to determine boundaries is geographically. You can use subdivision perimeters, city streets, or natural terrain. There are no rules. The boundaries can be any size, as long as they aren't so small or large to be counterproductive to the goals of the group and needs of the community. Ideally your boundaries should allow for response teams to be able to walk the area in a relatively short time to survey the damage and assess needs.

Organize the first meeting. Determine a time and place. Neighborhood meetings tend to be more successful when they are held *in* the neighborhood. Utilize someone's home, a church, library, community center, or any other available space that will accommodate the number of people you expect to attend. The overall atmosphere of these meetings can be negative, since the root of the gathering is crisis. Lighten the air by making it more social than business-like. Prepare snacks or coffee, maybe even an outdoor barbecue or potluck dinner.

Once you have organized your first meeting, you will want to distribute invitations. They can come in the form of social media, mailers, or fliers placed on neighborhood doors. Utilize any means you can to distribute the invitation and spread the word within your established boundaries. Hand delivery is most effective. "Cold calling" or going door to door can be off-putting to some, so consider other ways to deliver the invitation personally. Other neighborhood social events such as block parties can provide a good platform for you to begin garnering interest and distributing invitations.

THE FIRST MEETING

I would advise against inviting the "experts" to the first meeting. While their input and cooperation will be invaluable as you develop the group, the topic of disaster readiness and response can be overwhelming enough without the intimidation of badges and extensive resumes in the room. I would, though, find a point during the meeting to tell the group that you have established contacts with local emergency responders, stressing their involvement in meetings to come. This will give your idea and your group legitimacy.

Your first meeting should be inviting and informational. Introduce yourself and express what led you to call the meeting together. Tell them what sparked your interest in organizing the neighborhood and why you seek others with the same level of concern and willingness to help. The overtone should be more positive than negative, focusing on what you collectively have to offer rather than how bad circumstances can become. The primary objectives should be getting acquainted, educating, collecting information, and planning the next, larger meeting. Many groups have issued name tags to encourage getting to know one another and to establish and emphasize the initial social aspect of the meeting.

Invite others to introduce themselves and enlighten the group as to what brought them there and what they hope to achieve. Once introductions have been made, present a brief outline of your general disaster preparation-and-response goals for the neighborhood. It is important you know and relay to the other interested citizens that your ideas are not set in stone. They are mere topics for discussion. Encourage dialogue, questions, and ideas. Input from the members is critical for success and with it comes ownership, which will make this a true community endeavor.

You should have a form prepared for attendees to fill out basic information about them and other inhabitants of their house. Any information given on the sheet is absolutely voluntary and should be kept private within the group. The forms can be divided into two parts. The first part covers the household inhabitants and the second part covers the property. Include information such as the following:

Household Inhabitants

- Address
- Names and birthdates of occupants
- Phone numbers of occupants
- Email/social media contact info
- Employer
- Employer address and phone number
- What school the children attend
- School address and phone number
- School policy for release of children
- Person authorized to pick up children/contact info for authorized person
- Special skills/training/certifications
- Pertinent medical conditions/special needs
- Current medications
- Allergies
- Pets
- Pertinent pet information
- Out-of-area contacts

Property

- Address
- Owner/landlord contact information
- Family meeting place
- Contact info of those who have been given house keys or access codes
- Rough sketch of the home, identifying gas shut-off (G), water shut-off (W), electrical box (E), and other important information such as onsite hazardous materials, unique features, swimming pool, etc.
- Permission to turn off utilities if no one is home and to search the home if no one has been located

There is a lot of information contained in those forms and much of it is extremely personal. Participants, especially in the early stages of organizing the group, will likely be hesitant to offer personal information. That is OK. They will be more willing to offer it as the group grows and they see the benefit of having that information in a central and secure place. The biggest key to acquiring the information is not to push for it. Emphasize that it will not be for public consumption but kept in a safe place, accessed exclusively when there is a need to update or when an emergency occurs.

Make every attempt for the first meeting to be informative without being overwhelming. Before adjourning you should determine the date, location, and goals of the next meeting. The group must expand. Others are usually very receptive when they realize the difference their collective involvement can make in a coordinated response. Pass out informational pamphlets or documents that you have gathered from the fire department, Red Cross, etc., for attendees to read at home at their own leisure.

Finally, a few days after the initial meeting, send thank-you letters. The group could not exist without the volunteers that make it possible. Their attendance and input is invaluable. Include in the letter the date, time, and location of the next meeting along with a reminder of any duties to be done before then.

SUBSEQUENT MEETINGS

The first meeting was your opportunity to get to know one another and lay the groundwork for organizing a neighborhood emergency response group. There was likely a moderate turnout that left those in attendance with the desire to expand the group, gain training, and develop a plan. Subsequent meetings should see a growth in attendance as well as interest. Your discussion will begin to narrow from broad concepts to specific ideas and duties.

Offer those that are new a quick synopsis and history of the group up to that point. You don't want to rehash the first meeting every time, but as a courtesy and so as not to alienate new volunteers, a quick briefing that brings them up to speed would be appropriate. State, for the sake of first-timers and as a reminder to the regulars, group goals and priorities.

Begin to incorporate guest speakers. Representatives from the fire department or Red Cross can discuss how your group can assist them and offer tips for organization and training. When a speaker is not available, many organizations will offer a video or have media on their website that explains their role in a disaster and how neighborhood groups can help.

As the number of interested people begins to grow, you should develop strategies to promote individual and family preparedness. Task people with ensuring their own families and homes are ready for a crisis first. Encourage members to work together to offer help or suggestions. Once that occurs, neighborhood preparation and response coordination begins to grow organically.

IDENTIFYING NEIGHBORHOOD SKILLS AND RESOURCES

Every day, you move past your neighbors as you come and go. Sometimes you wave, sometimes you stop and talk, but oftentimes, you simply go on about your day giving little or no regard to those who live and work closest to you. These actions create no tangible benefit or consequence until you are forced to be self-sufficient.

During a time of crisis, wouldn't it be nice to know the woman a few houses down is a doctor, the man across the street is a military veteran with special search-and-rescue training, and the family on the next block has heavy equipment in a detached garage behind their house that they would offer in a disaster? Valuable resources in the form of equipment and skills can be found on every street in every community. In determining what assets you have at your disposal, you also determine deficits. Along with strengths will be weaknesses that should be identified. As you accumulate data, you will begin to see both.

As you form your neighborhood response group, one of the first orders of business will be to identify specific skill sets and equipment that can be used in a disaster. The aforementioned *assets* can take the form of a person, an object, a structure, a service, or anything else that could be utilized to improve the circumstances during a disaster.

Skill sets come with people. Some beneficial skills, such as medical training, are obvious. Others can benefit your response in different ways. A woodworker knows how to operate tools and could create or reinforce a structure. An accountant is good with documentation and can provide guidance with the ever-important record-keeping of the event. If you think about it, nearly every single person can provide something. Plumbers, cooks, pharmacists, psychologists, fire fighters, and architects all have something to offer and can be used in varying areas of need depending on their area of expertise.

Create a document or establish another way to determine what skills are present in your community and if those specialties are at your disposal. You would assume people are willing to help out during a disaster, but do not take for granted that just because you live next door to a doctor that the doctor would be willing to help. You must get their permission to be included in any planning. This will also prevent misconceptions. For example, "doctor" is a very broad statement, and what you assume is a medical doctor might actually be a psychologist. Both have their place and can be extremely beneficial, but one is not the other.

Also in that document or a separate one, identify equipment that can be used by the group. As with skills, the owners must be willing to allow its use. Equipment comes in all sizes and categories. You may want to separate the inventory into sections. Neighborhoods may have heavy equipment like front-end loaders. Smaller, common items like chainsaws, generators, ladders, shovels, and extension cords are kept in garages or sheds throughout the area and are needed in large quantities during a disaster response. Other items to consider logging in the group's inventory are:

- Axes
- Chains and rope
- Crow bars
- Extension cords
- First aid kits
- Generator
- Ham (amateur) radios
- Medical oxygen
- Portable lights
- Portable tables and chairs
- Shovels
- Walkie-talkies
- Wheelchairs
- Wheelbarrows
- Winches

Some equipment requires training or experience, so the owner may be needed to operate or possibly offer training for the group. Part of your role as a leader within the group is to ensure that the members can safely operate equipment. Consider training the group on the operation of hand tools, radios, and medical equipment to introduce safety and proficiency.

Finally, earmark structures and services like hospitals, churches, schools, and libraries that can be used as relocation or treatment areas during a disaster. You will, of course, need permission, but those types of occupancies will typically be more than happy to work with community groups to coordinate the use of their building and resources. You will want a location that is big enough to accommodate your needs. Sometimes, when no commercial structures are available, citizens offer up their homes, garages, and outbuildings. Services such as public transportation can offer assistance also. If they function in your area, learn their disaster response plan and how they can coordinate their assistance with the operations of your neighborhood group.

Once you have collected all of your asset information, it will be especially helpful to map that material for an easy-to-use visual aid when the need to locate something or someone arises. There are several ways to do this. One is to use a large street map. To avoid cluttering the map with information, use an accompanying folder with asset numbers that correlate to a number on the map.

For example, place a yellow dot with a number in it on the map where equipment you've obtained permission to use in a crisis is located. Place a blue dot with a number where a willing volunteer with a particular skill is located. In a corresponding book, you can reference the number to see the specific equipment or skill that is located there.

There is great debate over utilization versus overreliance on technology. Without question, computers, tablets, smartphones, etc., can be extremely valuable tools and hold vast amounts of information. If you choose to utilize them, several software programs and smartphone applications may be used. These programs are more sophisticated than paper maps and will allow you to create "overlay" maps that let you place one asset map over another and easily navigate between them. Another benefit of utilizing technology is the ability to attach pictures and even instructional videos with asset entries. There are some pitfalls, however, in maintaining a reliance on technology. Amid the devastation of the disaster, cellular towers needed to connect with the Internet and with other people, including emergency responders, may likely become damaged. The lines of communication are usually out of service due to destruction or can be overloaded in a frenzy of incoming and outgoing communication. Whichever method you choose, mapping your assets is a good idea that will simplify the process of locating them when you need them.

COMMAND STRUCTURE, JOB POSITIONS, AND DUTIES

Structure is inherent to every organization, committee, club, or group. An authority figure divides up responsibilities. With each responsibility, someone is in charge of people performing tasks. It is a coordinated effort that works within a command structure to provide safe, efficient, and comprehensive operations. Your neighborhood group should follow the same framework by establishing positions. I will discuss a few common job positions, but you can completely customize your group to best suit your needs. The only caveats are that your system must be functional and work well with emergency responders in your area. The command staff you set up can be as complex or as simple as the situation dictates. If you are prepared to staff the big scenario, the smaller one will be a breeze. Below you will learn some command staff positions, but your specific event might only require a handful of people and can be managed with a much smaller cache of participants and equipment. The following positions are merely examples. Customize your positions to meet your specific needs.

Coordinator. This position can also be called "leader" or "incident commander." In all honesty, you can call the person the "top chief in charge" or "supreme ruler" if you want. It doesn't really matter as long as everyone in the system knows who is in charge and what terminology you are using. The coordinator will be the leader of your neighborhood group and act as a liaison between your group and other groups, as well as emergency responders. He or she will basically be the "face" of your neighborhood group. The coordinator will:

- Monitor the coordination and training of your neighborhood group
- Develop working relationships with other groups and outside agencies
- Ensure neighborhood information is gathered, recorded, accessible, and current
- Relay information to the local fire department or appropriate agency during a disaster
- Organize team leaders
- Establish, with team leaders, a plan of action and monitor disaster-response operations

Liaison. This person serves as the unofficial workhouse of the group. The liaison works between the coordinator and neighborhood residents to organize meetings, as well as ensure residents and teams have the information, supplies, and a disaster strategy needed to function during a crisis. The liaison will:

- Organize meetings

- Identify new residents and make contact with them to see if they would be interested in joining
- Note potential problems in the area
- Put residents in contact with each other to fill any deficiencies or needs
- Act as the coordinator in his or her absence
- Ensure accurate and current information is passed between coordinator and teams during a disaster
- Coordinates a neighborhood survey to determine damage and needs

Team leader. During a disaster, volunteers will be divided up into teams. Examples might be search teams, rescue teams, triage teams, treatment teams, utilities teams, animal rescue teams, etc. A team leader is just as the title implies. That person will be in charge of one to seven people to perform an assigned task. As any good leader will tell you, in their absence, if they've done their job, someone else should be able to fill in and perform their functions. A team leader must ensure that the members of his or her team are prepared to perform the tasks they are assigned as well as be able to lead if necessary. Team leaders will:

- Train as necessary for the position and specific tasks
- Develop a functional plan for the team during a disaster
- Maintain the ability to communicate and coordinate with other teams
- Identify and take inventory of equipment and supplies needed for his or her job assignment and those needed by the teams
- Report information about the event, team members, activities, supplies, equipment, and needs to the liaison or coordinator

Someone always runs the show and is ultimately responsible. At work, at school, and yes, even at home, there is always someone in charge. Your neighborhood "command structure" should mimic that of a fire department or military operation, meaning that everyone has a clearly defined role and specific responsibilities. The person in charge shouldn't be the loudest or the person who raises their hand first. Ideally, it is someone with experience, leadership qualities, and the ability to stay cool under pressure. People will naturally gravitate toward certain positions within the structure. Some will naturally fill a leadership role, and others will be the ones putting bandages on the wounded. Both are vitally important and their roles should be filled by those who best serve the purpose.

MOBILIZATION AND WORKING WITHIN THE INCIDENT MANAGEMENT SYSTEM

You've laid the groundwork. You have been working with local agencies and have created a neighborhood emergency response team. People in your neighborhood have stepped up and volunteered to be a part of the solution to a sizable problem. Your team has attended meetings, taken training classes, taken inventory of safety equipment, and has a general idea of what individual roles will be when a disaster occurs. Then it does.

An event happens right in your neighborhood. What event, you ask? Fill in the blank. It is only a minor detail because whatever happened has crippled your neighborhood and left you in the worst-case scenario that you had been preparing for. The first thing you can expect is to be overwhelmed with the "I can't believe this just happened" feeling. Then, it's time to take action.

Take account of specific priorities, in the following order, when handling any concerns in the wake of the event:

1. Yourself

2. Your family

3. Your home

4. Your immediate neighbors

5. Your response team

Evaluate yourself and ensure that you are OK and capable of rendering aid to others. Is everyone else in your house OK? Once you determine the medical condition of yourself and family, check your home. Investigate the structure and shut off any utilities that are already or could become problematic. Do the same for your immediate neighbors, and then you are ready to join the team.

You should have already established a meeting place where your neighborhood group is to mobilize. Maybe it is the home of the coordinator. Maybe it is the high school. It doesn't matter, as long as your group knows the location and it is safe for you to assemble there. In training, your group should have been told to self-activate. Do not wait for a phone call or secret signal. Chances are telecommunication will be hindered and likely not even possible after the event. Once the individuals have their own family, home, and immediate neighbors take care of, they should automatically report to the "command center."

Team members should bring their own prepared PPE and safety equipment. Bring sturdy footwear, gloves, safety glasses, weather-appropriate clothing, a hard hat and respirator, if available, first aid kits, flashlights, and any other items that can be used and safely carried.

Once people begin to assemble, the coordinator or incident commander will begin setting up the command structure. First and foremost, if possible, the coordinator should advise local dispatch (usually 911) that there is a neighborhood response team assembled and where the command center is located. Knowing that a system is in place and operations are already in progress saves a lot of time when emergency crews are able to respond.

Fire departments around the country follow what is called the Incident Command System (ICS). The ICS is a structured command system that keeps individuals working within their span of control, which usually entails being in charge of five people or fewer. Your neighborhood command structure could mimic the fire command structure, though it doesn't have to follow it exactly. As with a formal ICS, your system can expand or shrink to fit the needs of the event.

At a large-scale incident, the fire service, under the incident commander, identifies four categories of needs and places one person in charge of each of them: finance, logistics, operations, and planning (often remembered as FLOP). There probably won't be much for a "finance" person to do in your response group, so you could eliminate that from your structure right away. Your primary areas will be operations and planning.

NIMS VERSUS ICS

NIMS stands for the National Incident Management System and is a program of the Federal Emergency Management Agency (FEMA). NIMS offers a comprehensive approach to the coordination of disaster management and is responsible for coordinating disaster response on city, state, and federal levels.

ICS is the Incident Command System. The ICS is a management structure used to control disaster response. When properly implemented, ICS can establish a chain of command of any size to accommodate a crisis. It standardizes on-scene management.

NIMS offers training in ICS to provide a structured framework that allows various agencies to coordinate command during a disaster. The "command structure" you build in your neighborhood emergency response group should follow ICS, which offers the benefit of common terminology and an ease of process as command transfers operations from your initial response group to responding agencies.

It can be difficult to plan for a specific number of neighborhood responders. Sometimes, far fewer people than you expected show up due to the time of day (for example an afternoon when people are typically at work or school) or damage sustained to their homes. There may even be more than you expected as people rally to help one another. For the sake of planning, let's assume you have enough people to run a full-blown disaster response.

Your coordinator will begin to assemble teams: search, rescue, medical, etc., placing one person in charge of each. That way, 15 searchers won't all try to communicate at once. There will be three five-person teams, with one person in charge of each talking only to the people under his or her span of control. Ideally you would have established a means of communicating prior the event, but if not, one should be determined before sending the teams out.

Accountability can become a major problem at a large-scale incident. In the command structure, several people should have the job of tracking volunteer helpers. Believe me, it sounds easier than it is. This can be one of the most difficult and important jobs at the scene. The area will be in chaos and people will be in near panic as they come and go. Maintaining accountability will be a monumental task and emergency responders, as they arrive on scene, will want to have access to that information right away.

As emergency responders, most likely the fire department, begin to arrive, they will not simply take over operations. You would have already established a relationship so they will know there is a response team in the area where your command center is located. The truth is, emergency responders would rather you not be there. Reading that sentence may sting a little bit, but it is the truth. They are well-trained in all areas of the response. They have a history of working together within a well-defined command structure and know that the person working alongside them has received the same training and possesses roughly the same skills. When they show up to your neighborhood, they never know what to expect. There are varying levels of proficiency, accountability, knowledge, and skills from neighborhood to neighborhood and person to person. They would rather handle the situation themselves from the beginning to provide as safe and efficient an operation as possible.

Having said that, they can't be there from the beginning and will appreciate the fact that you have been. If you have done your job in preparing, assembling, and activating the people of your neighborhood, your local emergency responders should arrive at your command center, receive a briefing, and then work with you as operations transition to them. From experience I can tell you that volunteer rescuers who are doing a good job will be left in place in the absence of professional help.

COMMUNITY EMERGENCY RESPONSE TEAMS

With the growing recognition and acknowledgment of the many benefits that a community caring for itself in the moments, hours, and days following a disaster can provide, the federal government decided to formalize the curriculum. In 1993, FEMA made the Community Emergency Response Team (CERT) educational program available nationally. CERT, originally developed by the Los Angeles Fire Department in the mid-80s, increases community understanding that there is a need for citizens to be professionally trained, adequately prepared, and formally organized. According to the FEMA website, since its inception, CERT has been taught to communities in 28 states and Puerto Rico.

Several offshoots of the program, such as Neighborhood Emergency Response Training (NERT) and individualized Incident Response Teams (IRT) and Emergency Response Teams (ERT) have developed. FEMA and multiple other online sources will inform you if there is an ERT in your area. They all base their curriculum on neighborhood preparedness and practical skills designed to empower people to recognize potential threats and do what is needed to lessen the effects on themselves, their families, and the community.

Being connected with a trained group that shares a common goal empowers communities. CERT offers basic training, continuing education, and affiliation. Most communities choose to follow the basic training provided by FEMA, customizing training and practical exercises to fit the needs of their members and response area.

If a CERT is not already available in your area and you are interested in starting one, FEMA offers guidance in a single document that expands on several of the concepts covered in this book. The document on the step-by-step processes of starting and maintaining a CERT covers:

CERT Overview
CERT roles

- Step 1: Assessing needs
- Step 2: Identifying resources
- Step 3: Gaining support and recruiting
- Step 4: Acquiring training materials
- Step 5: Tailoring training
- Step 6: Establishing a training cadre
- Step 7: Delivering training

Maintaining a CERT

- Step 1: Communicating with volunteers
- Step 2: Maintaining partnerships
- Step 3: Planning and continuing training
- Step 4: Maintaining records

CERT programs are very popular around the country and extremely useful in community disaster preparation when disaster strikes. Look into programs in your community or utilize this book and online resources made available by FEMA to start your own CERT. It might be the most important thing (and possibly the most fun) you can have in your community.

SUMMARY

Assuming the responsibility of developing a neighborhood response group is a respectable endeavor. You recognize the potential and want to take steps to ensure the safety of your family and those around you. It can be time-consuming and often frustrating and daunting. It will also be rewarding in ways that you couldn't begin to preconceive. You will find that a common purpose like preparing your neighborhood to be self-sufficient will bring a community together. Strangers become teammates and friends. Meetings become training sessions and blossom into social events. A neighborhood allied in purpose lends itself to the best possible outcome in the wake of a disaster.

Within your neighborhood you will find equipment and skills that you never knew were present. As you organize them, acknowledge what you have and seek out what you don't. Look for voids in your available inventory and skill sets. You will be surprised at what you have available and concerned by what you don't. As a group you can obtain those things, filling the gaps to better meet the goals you set forth. Organize, train, work with your local municipalities, and prepare your neighborhood to take care of each other.

CONCLUSION

This book may have left you feeling a little bit overwhelmed and, if I've done my job, perhaps motivated to begin taking steps to ensure you are prepared and able to respond when the unthinkable happens. With years of experience racing to the aid of others in the big red fire truck, I can tell you it doesn't take much for circumstances to demand more than emergency responders can adequately provide. Communities are protected as well as they can be within the confines of a budget and the projected demand for emergency services. It simply isn't financially viable for municipalities to keep a full-time staff for the rare major event. But, to be sure, those major events happen and when they do, citizens don't choose to handle situations themselves—they are forced to.

The previous chapters targeted subjects that are critical and common to a wide range of catastrophes. In many cases, the specific event that occurred is merely a detail. Regardless of the cause, survivors are forced to encounter commonalities among the spectrum of man-made and natural disasters. The principal concern across the board is life safety.

Unfortunately, lives are often taken during the actual event, but it is in the time frame following it that critical decisions are made and lives saved and lost. Survivors feel an obligation to help other survivors and, fueled by adrenaline and anxiety, put themselves at great risk to help others. By taking the time to preplan a coordinated response, you greatly reduce the exposure of volunteer rescuer injury and death.

Though you should educate yourself about what disasters your area is prone to, know that you should be ready for a variety of catastrophes. No one singular threat is common to everyone. Of the deadliest disasters in US history, the top ten list includes four tropical cyclones, an earthquake and fire, a terrorist attack, a military strike, a dam that burst, a shipwreck, and a heat wave. The remainder of the list is filled with tornados, floods, fires, and a variety of other catastrophic events, emphasizing the benefits that a broad outlook toward your training and preparation can have.

While I was teaching a community response group, a student once asked me where to begin. The information, supplies, preparation, and training seemed mountainous and intimidating. She said she didn't even know what she didn't know. One man in the class interjected that he felt the exact same way at first. He began by imagining he was going camping. If he and his family were going to be away from their home and "roughing it" for a week, what would he need for supplies, clothing, or food? So he began with basic items like extra clothing, food, and water. Then, if they were in the wilderness and the weather turned on them, what would he like to have to keep them safe and protected? He added first aid supplies, tarps, and tools. Then he thought about how he would keep his kids entertained without electricity and how he would make sure their family dog was also safe. From that point his home supplies began to gradually increase as did his desire for information. He wanted to learn first aid, how to work a fire extinguisher, and other such skills. From his perspective, if he had the supplies and knowledge to care for his family, then he had the supplies and knowledge to care for his community too. For him, the secret to getting started was to plan a camping trip.

It is truly a mindset. Don't expect to read this book or take a CPR class and magically become qualified to manage a disaster. There is a reason that firefighters, police officers, soldiers, paramedics, and others continually train. Ability requires the opportunity to grow; otherwise it decays. I shudder to compare my skill level and knowledge base as a firefighter today with that of my first day on the job or the day I hopped on that rig to respond to my first emergency call. As the student in the class felt, I was completed intimidated on my first day as a firefighter. The information, supplies, preparation, and training *were* mountainous. Like her, I didn't even know what I didn't know until I talked to the guys who had been on the job for years. At that time, I could not imagine being trained and ready for basically anything and everything. I was suddenly unsure of myself and my ability to be ready for the tasks being required of me. I reverted back to the question and answer I heard somewhere in life long before when I was up against something seemingly insurmountable. How do you eat an elephant? One bite at a time.

Maybe you are like the student in the class with nothing more than a desire to be prepared and help others, or maybe you have vast experience with managing crisis. In either case, a successful neighborhood response presents unique challenges and rewards. The bottom line is, people will help people. It's what we do and have done throughout history. But to provide the greatest good to the greatest number of people and in the safest way possible for volunteer responders, safety and coordination are paramount. Remember that disregarding rescuer safety only exasperates the problem.

Take this book chapter by chapter and make notes, ask questions, seek answers, and use it as a springboard for your own training and preparation. This, by no means, is all-encompassing. Only you know what your specific needs are—your strengths and weaknesses, your resources and deficits.

Most of all, reach out. Talk to people. Find others in your area that are as interested as you are about disaster readiness. Locate the experts and get their insight. Make a coordinated plan. Create a network to make sure your community can take care of each other. That is what it is all about: a collective effort in which a group of people band together to ensure each other's safety. Take care of yourself and each other and you will afford yourself the best-possible outcome of the worst-possible scenario.

The following is a summary of some of the main points of the previous chapters. A "cheat sheet," if you will. Use this to glean discussion points or, as your proficiency grows, as a reminder.

QUICK REFERENCE GUIDE

INCIDENT PRIORITIES

- ❑ Life safety
- ❑ Incident stabilization
- ❑ Property conservation

9 STEPS OF SIZE-UP

- ❑ Gather facts
- ❑ Assess damage
- ❑ Consider probabilities
- ❑ Assess your situation
- ❑ Establish priorities
- ❑ Make decisions
- ❑ Develop a plan of action
- ❑ Take action
- ❑ Evaluate progress

UTILITY SHUT-OFF

Water

- ❑ Locate water shut-off valve (typically where the water line enters the foundation).
- ❑ Turn valve until it is perpendicular to the pipe, or twist it clockwise until you can't turn it anymore.

Electricity

- ❑ If electrical panel is damaged or there is standing water near the breaker box, evacuate immediately and deny entry.
- ❑ Locate main electrical breaker box, often in a basement or utility room.
- ❑ Flip the breaker labeled "main" to the off position (this may be a push button breaker in older homes).
- ❑ If there is no "main" breaker, switch all breakers to the off position.

Gas

- ❑ If you hear hissing or smell gas, evacuate immediately and deny entry.
- ❑ Locate the gas meter, typically found outside near the house.
- ❑ Locate the shut-off valve between the meter and the house. Using an emergency gas shut-off wrench or a crescent wrench, turn the valve until it is perpendicular to the pipe.
- ❑ Gas should only be turned back on by a professional.

EVACUATION PREPAREDNESS

- ❑ Identify potential hazards.
- ❑ Determine evacuation routes.
- ❑ Designate a meeting place.
- ❑ Have an accountability system in place.

DISASTER COMMUNICATION PLAN

- ❑ Establish an out-of-town point of contact.
- ❑ Notify family and friends of your point of contact.
- ❑ Ensure all contact information for family and friends is up to date and correct. Give this list to your point of contact.
- ❑ Put a laminated "contact card" in your child's backpack with your contact information as well as that of your out-of-town contact.
- ❑ Quality check contact information annually.

DISASTER PROCEDURE

Flood

- ❑ Heed all appropriate flood warnings issued by authorities.
- ❑ Move important items to higher floors in the structure.
- ❑ Turn off utilities and unplug electrical equipment.
- ❑ Secure your home by locking all doors and windows.
- ❑ Evacuate to a safe location using a predetermined route.
- ❑ Avoid traversing moving water.
- ❑ Avoid contact with flood water; it is often toxic.
- ❑ Be aware of downed power lines.
- ❑ Avoid stray animals, as they may be aggressive.

Storms

- ❑ Go inside and stay there until the storm passes.
- ❑ Know outdoor safety procedures in the event you can't get indoors.
- ❑ Determine if it is safer to stay in or bug out.
- ❑ Avoid contact with electrical equipment and plumbing during a storm.
- ❑ Avoid windows.
- ❑ Bring pets inside and safely secure them until the storm is over.

Blizzards

- ❏ Monitor the weather.
- ❏ Stay where you are.
- ❏ Localize your heat to as small an area as possible.
- ❏ Keep walking surfaces clear.
- ❏ Know the signs and symptoms of hypothermia.
- ❏ Check on your neighbors.
- ❏ Be careful of dangers hidden in accumulated snow.
- ❏ If you're in your vehicle when a storm hits, do not leave it.

Earthquakes

- ❏ Go to a predetermined safe area.
- ❏ Drop, cover, and hold on.
- ❏ If you're in bed, cover your head with a pillow and stay in bed.
- ❏ Remain indoors.
- ❏ Expect to hear building and car alarms.
- ❏ Avoid power lines.
- ❏ If you're in a vehicle at the time of the earthquake, pull over to a safe area.

Tornados

- ❏ Monitor the weather.
- ❏ Go to a safe place.
- ❏ Leash or crate your pets and bring them to your safe place.
- ❏ If you're in your car, drive to the nearest safe area and remain in the vehicle, covering your head.
- ❏ If you are outside, get in as low an area as possible and cover your body with anything you can find.
- ❏ Avoid overpasses.

Civil Unrest

❑ Monitor local media for situational updates.

❑ If you have advance notice, leave the area.

❑ If there is no time to evacuate, barricade yourself in (while allowing yourself a way out).

❑ Be prepared for gunfire, physical violence, and fires.

❑ Avoid public areas.

❑ Keep a level head and a low profile.

THE FOUR ELEMENTS OF FIRE

❑ Heat

❑ Fuel

❑ Oxygen

❑ Chemical reaction

CLASSES OF FIRE

❑ Class A (green triangle): ordinary combustibles such as wood, paper, and cloth

❑ Class B (red square): flammable liquids

❑ Class C (blue circle): energized electrical equipment

❑ Class D (yellow star): combustible metals

❑ Class K (black hexagon): cooking oils

FIRE EXTINGUISHER OPERATION

❑ Pull

❑ Aim

❑ Squeeze

❑ Sweep

DAMAGE ASSESSMENT

- ❏ Light damage: superficial
- ❏ Moderate damage: visible signs of structural damage
- ❏ Heavy damage: obvious structural instability

BUILDING SEARCH LAYOUT: A, B, C, D METHOD

- ❏ Side A: front or "address" side
- ❏ Side B: the side to the left as you're facing side A
- ❏ Side C: the back of the structure
- ❏ Side D: the other side

SEARCH MARKINGS

- ❏ Mark a slash near the door of the search area.
- ❏ In the left or 9 o'clock quadrant, write your name or agency group.
- ❏ In the upper quadrant, write the date and time you enter.
- ❏ Complete the "X" as you exit the search area.
- ❏ In the upper quadrant, write the date and time you leave.
- ❏ In the right or 3 o'clock quadrant, note the areas of the structure that were searched and specific hazard information.
- ❏ In the lower or 6 o'clock quadrant, enter information regarding victims found in the search area.

ONE-PERSON CARRIES

- ❏ One-person walk assist
- ❏ Cradle-in-arms carry
- ❏ Arm carry
- ❏ Firefighter carry
- ❏ Pack strap carry

TWO-PERSON CARRIES

❑ Two-person walk assist
❑ Chair carry
❑ Two-person extremity carry
❑ Two-handed seat carry
❑ Four-handed seat carry

DRAGS

❑ Shoulder drag
❑ Blanket drag
❑ Feet drag

TRIAGE

❑ Green: minor injuries
❑ Yellow: delayed treatment
❑ Red: immediate treatment
❑ Black: deceased

RPM PATIENT ASSESSMENT

❑ Respirations: 12 to 20 breaths per minute
❑ Perfusion: 2-second capillary refill
❑ Mental status: can answer simple questions

CHECK ABCS

❑ Airway: shake and check for responsiveness
❑ Breathing: look, listen, and feel
❑ Circulation: check for a pulse

BLEEDING CONTROL TREATMENT

- ❏ Direct pressure
- ❏ Elevation
- ❏ Bandage and sterile dressing

SHOCK TREATMENT

- ❏ Lie the victim on their back.
- ❏ Evaluate their ABCs.
- ❏ Control bleeding if necessary.
- ❏ Elevate the feet 6 to 12 inches.
- ❏ Loosen clothing.
- ❏ Provide cooling or warmth to keep the victim comfortable.
- ❏ Seek professional medical care as soon as possible.

PHYSICAL SYMPTOMS OF TRAUMA

- ❏ Chest pain
- ❏ Diarrhea
- ❏ Fatigue
- ❏ Headache
- ❏ Hyperactivity
- ❏ Loss of appetite
- ❏ Nightmares
- ❏ Sleep disturbances
- ❏ Stomach pain or nausea

PSYCHOLOGICAL SYMPTOMS OF TRAUMA

❑ Fear of reoccurrence

❑ Feelings of helplessness

❑ Inability to concentrate

❑ Increased alcohol or drug consumption

❑ Irritability

❑ Isolation or withdrawal

❑ Mood swings

❑ Numbness

❑ Relationship strife

❑ Sadness or depression

❑ Self-blame

DISASTER PREPAREDNESS NETWORKS

❑ Identify preexisting groups in your community or the lack of.

❑ Organize a group of like-minded individuals to assist you.

❑ Establish goals, determine boundaries, and organize the first meeting of your community disaster response team.

❑ Identify neighborhood skills and resources.

❑ Establish a command structure, job positions, and duties.

❑ Make contact with local authorities and determine how your neighborhood group can assist and fit within their command structure during a major event.

PHOTO CREDITS

ACKNOWLEDGMENTS

I would like to thank all at Ulysses Press for their vision and hard work on this book, particularly Keith Riegert and Jake Flaherty. To my sons: Ryan, Nick, and Cameron. My family, both near and far, who have always provided unwavering love and support. My Overland Park Fire Department family. Scott B. Williams, to whom I am forever indebted. To all who provided input, suggestions, or other forms of support for this book: Michelle Brenner, Tricia Roberts, Jason Rhodes, Richie Finazzo, Cameron Finazzo, Amy Finazzo, Mike Huff, Micah Jensen, Terra Moriarty, Xavier Panimboza, Doug Hall, and Mike Morgan.

ABOUT THE AUTHOR

Scott Finazzo, like his father before him, has been a firefighter for nearly 20 years and currently serves as a lieutenant for the Overland Park (Kansas) Fire Department. He has been an instructor for community emergency response teams since 2000, helping to educate and prepare citizens for emergencies. In addition to being an emergency responder and educator, Scott has been writing in various capacities for much of his life, contributing to blogs, magazines, and books. Scott's first book, *The Prepper's Workbook*, coauthored with Scott B. Williams, became a national best seller. He followed that up with *Why Do All the Locals Think We're Crazy?*, a narrative of his kayaking journey through the Virgin Islands.

With years of experience both preparing for and responding to disasters, he has developed a keen interest in survival. Scott's self-reliance skills have been honed by forays into the mountains and deserts of America, in, on, and under the ocean, and by several excursions into islands of the Caribbean. He maintains an intrinsic connection to travel and adventure, documenting many of his endeavors on his site: www.lureofthehorizon.com.

Scott has a bachelor's degree in management and human relations and two associate's degrees. He currently lives in Shawnee, Kansas, until he can establish himself somewhere among palm trees. Find more on Scott's website, www.scottfinazzo.com.